MARITAL PATHOLOGY

An Introduction for
Doctors, Counsellors and Clergy

JACK DOMINIAN

Articles published in
the *British Medical Journal*

Darton, Longman & Todd
British Medical Association
LONDON

Published in Great Britain in 1980

Darton, Longman & Todd Ltd
89 Lillie Road
London SW6 1UD
and
British Medical Association
Tavistock Square
London WC1H 9JR

© British Medical Journal 1979

ISBN 0 232 51479 8 (DLT)
     0 7279 0061 7 (BMA)

Printed in Great Britain by The Anchor Press Ltd
and bound by Wm Brendon & Son Ltd
both of Tiptree, Essex

Contents

		Page
Foreword	.. ..	iv
Preface	.. ..	v
1 Health and marital breakdown	.. ..	1
2 Definition and extent of marital pathology	.. ..	6
3 Social factors and marital pathology	.. .. ..	10
4 Choice of partner	.. ..	14
5 First phase of marriage	.. ..	19
6 Second phase of marriage	.. ..	26
7 Third phase of marriage	.. ..	33
8 Marriage and psychiatric illness	.. ..	39
9 Management: Basic counselling	.. ..	44
10 Management: Psychodynamics	.. ..	49
11 Management: Sexual counselling	.. ..	54

Foreword

by the Editor
British Medical Journal

In 1772 Dr Johnson said: "It is so far from being natural for a man and a woman to live in a state of marriage, that we all find the motives that they have for remaining in that connection, and the restraints which civilised society imposes to prevent separation, are hardly sufficient to keep them together." Divorce was introduced in England and Wales in 1857. Since then over four million people have been divorced and, at current rates, some six million more will divorce in the remaining years of this century. As Dr J Dominian explains in this book, the same pattern is seen in every Western society. Every doctor, indeed every health worker, will increasingly see the effects of marital pathology, and yet few have had any special training in dealing with the problems. Dr Dominian, in a way that can be understood by all, describes the problems that can beset a marriage, how these problems can affect the health of the whole family, and how a general practitioner or any other counsellor can help an unhappy couple. This book deserves to be widely read.

STEPHEN LOCK
December 1979

Preface

The description given to human behaviour which involves medicine, social services, and the law simultaneously is social pathology. Such problems as alcoholism, drug addiction, delinquency, psychosexual difficulties, are readily recognised nowadays as belonging to this group of social disturbance and a great quantity of resources has been directed towards their alleviation.

Marital breakdown has not been recognised as a condition which belongs to social pathology. Indeed, there are some who would violently oppose the whole concept that there is anything pathological in marital breakdown. It is considered an entirely private affair for the members of the family concerned.

And yet there is an enormous amount of distress involving the spouses. There is marital stress and ill health, a tenfold increase in suicide risk, a recourse to alcohol for succour, and a good deal of psychosomatic illness. The children are involved in pain which is not of their choice and also experience variable amounts of distress. All this disturbance seeks relief, and the doctor, social worker, health visitor, the clergy, teacher, and marriage counsellor are regularly confronted with requests for help.

This series of articles which appeared in the British Medical Journal in Autumn 1979 is an attempt to introduce workers in the field to one framework of reference regarding marital problems. Initially addressed to medical students and doctors, the contents are of interest to other professional groups dealing with marriage problems. These articles, supplemented by the author's Penguin, *Marital Breakdown*, are an attempt to offer an introductory work in this complex field. There are other, more advanced, textbooks which take the interested reader further, such as, H. V. Dicks, *Marital Tensions* and A. C. R. Skynner, *One Flesh: Separate Persons*.

When some half-a-million men, women, and children are currently involved in divorce annually, and with no sign of reduction of the size

Preface

of the problem, there is a pressing need to offer effective help to many who need it urgently. I hope that this little book will be of assistance.

I would like to thank the British Medical Journal for publishing the articles, and for their co-operation with my publishers, Darton, Longman & Todd, to make the material available to a wider audience.

J. DOMINIAN

Central Middlesex Hospital
December 1979

1   Health and marital breakdown

At first thought, marriage may seem unconnected to the practice of medicine. But marital breakdown, which is increasingly common, is the source of an enormous amount of unhappiness and illness. Marital problems present in diverse ways to almost all doctors, as well as to counsellors, the clergy, relatives, and friends. In this book the causes, the effects, and the management of marital breakdown will all be considered.

PROBLEMS BEFORE MARRIAGE

Premarital problems are only a tiny proportion of all the problems related to marriage. Genetic advice may be sought before marriage. Venereal disease and sexual difficulties encountered in courtship may present to the doctor; contraceptive advice may also be wanted.

One distinct condition that the doctor may meet is engagement neurosis, or engyesis, which is characterised by anxiety, depression, and appreciable hesitation about the pending marriage. One study showed that after five years half of these patients were married, but that a quarter of the original group, whether married or not, continued to have fluctuating ill health.[1]

DISSOLUTION OF AFFECTIVE BOND

Bowlby has shown how we form our first affectionate bonds with our parents, and that the consequences of the bond breaking are anxiety, anger, and depression.[2][3] This capacity to form strong bonds with others continues in adult life. In courtship a person selects one particular partner and forms an affective bond. The bond continues and intensifies with marriage itself, which in our society is conventionally an exclusive and permanent relationship. When this bond is threatened and seems likely to break, then, just as in infancy, a sequence of searching, protest, despair, and detachment—all accompanied by anxiety, anger, and depression—may be expected.

Most couples can cope with an expected separation. When the departure is unexpected, it usually leads to searching accompanied by anxiety and anger. Frantic telephoning and inquiring continue until the partner is found. Then follows strong protest, which may consist of shouting, crying, or screaming. Every practitioner has seen agitated, weeping patients who are occasionally drunk and sometimes have swallowed a handful of tablets and who are unhappily seeking help to bring back the departed partner. This is the adult imitation of the distressed young child who has temporarily lost its mother. If the mother does not return the child goes beyond the phase of search, protest, and despair to that of detachment. Similarly, after the searching, anxiety, anger, and depression, the deserted partner will progress slowly to detachment. Gradually, over months or years, the attachment ceases to exist. It is then—and then only—that the emotional link between the couple ceases. Anxious and hurtful exchanges give way to cool, indifferent, and even friendly remarks. This prolonged stress may be experienced privately or medical help may be sought. Marital pathology has become a common problem presenting to the doctor.

A study of psychiatric illness in several urban practices showed that marital problems were the factor most commonly associated with psychiatric illness. Women were more often affected than men.[4] The authors ask why marital difficulties should be so predominantly a female problem. "Though such difficulties must concern both marital partners, husbands consult less frequently on this score." The reasons for this are multiple. Women are sensitive to marital problems that their husbands do not recognise. The difficulty often has to become pronounced before the husband becomes aware of the problem. Even then husbands believe that marital difficulties are a private problem that is rarely serious enough to bother the doctor. Often the husband refuses to act, and blames his wife, who in seeking help becomes the scapegoat. Wives may seek help to reassure themselves that they are not going "mad", as is often suggested by husbands who refuse to face the marital difficulty.

PSYCHOSOMATIC AND PSYCHOLOGICAL SYMPTOMS

Patients may either ask for help directly for a marital problem, or indirectly by offering physical or psychological symptoms. Some patients find it easier to present a physical symptom, which may disguise the real problem. Patients, of course, are not frauds: they are genuinely seeking help and the doctor must lead them from the symptoms to the marital problems. Psychosomatic symptoms are often pre-eminent: attacks of breathlessness, difficulty in breathing, pain in the chest, or aggravation of asthma; pain over the heart or palpitations; abdominal pains, feelings of nausea, and changes in bowel rhythm, usually diarrhoea; headaches, fainting attacks, paraesthesia, hot and cold feelings; frequency, dysuria, backache, and sexual problems; or loss of hair and pruritus. Nasopharyngeal complaints are also commonly mentioned.

The patient presenting with psychological symptoms will usually be suffering from anxiety, a depressive illness, or a mixture of the two. The full anxiety attack will show physical manifestations of palpitations, breathlessness, flushing, sweating, insomnia, fatigue, and more psychological manifestations—of apprehension, fear, irritability, agitation, restlessness, and inability to concentrate—with or without specific phobic, obsessional, or hysterical symptoms. When depressed, the patient's mood may be anxious, but often tends towards misery with overt weeping and, if the depression deepens, indifference to life, people, and things. They may feel suicidal. The depression may be accompanied by severe insomnia, diurnal variation of mood, loss of energy, appetite, sexual desire, and weight, and an inability to remember, concentrate, or even work.

Depression is one of the commonest responses to marital stress. It may occur in the acute phase of marital difficulties, during the period of separation or divorce, and sometimes continue after the divorce. In a retrospective study of 150 women, a proportion of a much larger sample who petitioned for divorce, no fewer than 130 complained of symptoms suggestive of depression, and the remaining 20 mentioned symptoms but did not consider them a disturbance of health.[5] The 130 women who complained of symptoms mentioned, in order of frequency: crying, weight change, sleep disturbance, tiredness, lack of concentration, increased smoking, self-neglect, and drinking. The symptoms are most severe during the latter part of the marriage and during the early separation, when an attachment still exists but is under threat. The association of separation, divorce, and depressive illness has been confirmed in other studies.[6] Recently other studies have paid attention to life events that may trigger depressive or schizophrenic disorders. Some have shown that marital disruption and divorce carry a high probability of starting a depressive illness.[7]

SUICIDAL ATTEMPTS

Suicidal attempts are associated with marital pathology. A study of self-poisoning in 68 married men and 147 married women showed that marital disharmony was a major precipitating factor in 68% of the men and 60% of the women. Some 30% of the marriages of the men and 26% of the women had broken down, and in 17% the break-up had been within a month of the suicidal attempt.[8] In a selection of 130 people, taken from a wider sample of 577 cases in Oxford, 83% of the married men and 68% of the women complained of marital problems.[9] Three features stood out in this study. Firstly, during the previous twelve months, half of the married men and a tenth of the married women had had an extramarital affair. Secondly, the event most frequently related to the suicide attempt was a quarrel with a key person; this had occurred seven days before the attempt in 48% of cases and mostly in the two days before. Thirdly, separation from a key person was the most common precipitating event in those under 20. Those who repeat their suicide attempts are most likely to ultimately kill themselves. In a study of 204 patients with a history of repeated suicide attempts, separation or divorce, or both,[10] was one of the features present—a finding confirmed in another study.[11]

The exact incidence of suicide in society is unknown. It has never-

Health and marital breakdown

theless been estimated that throughout the world at least 1000 people commit suicide daily—half a million people dying each year is a reasonable estimate.[12] Figures computed first for West Sussex and Portsmouth for 1968 and also for England and Wales for 1970 give some remarkable results (B M Baraclough, personal communication). The suicide rate per 100 000 of the population over the age of 15 in West Sussex and Portsmouth is shown in the table. The highest rate is in those who are married but living apart: those who have not resolved their affectional bond, are isolated, and have yet to reconstruct their life. This trend is also shown in the figures for England and Wales, where the suicide rates for the married are 7·8 per 100 000, rising to 11·1 for the single, 23·9 for the widowed, and 35·5 for the divorced. An important clinical finding is that the vulnerable state of being separated and divorced is aggravated by the existence of children.[13]

TABLE I—*Effect of marital state on suicide rate in West Sussex and Portsmouth*

Marital state	Suicide rate/ 100 000 population
Married	9·9
Single	16·3
Widowed	16·3
Divorced	47·9
Married but living apart	204.4

HEALTH OF CHILDREN

Young children whose parents are experiencing severe marital distress may show the whole range of physical symptoms including disorders of sleep, feeding, and elimination; aggravation of any psychosomatic disorder such as asthma, abdominal pains, and headaches; and attention seeking, clinging, and crying.

Recent research has highlighted the presence of behavioural problems in children experiencing parental stress. This has been shown in preschool children who are the offspring of marriages characterised by frequent arguments, disagreements about the children, failure to make combined decisions, and low satisfaction on the mother's part with the help received from her husband.[14] The same behavioural disorder is found, associated with marital discord, in older children.[15] [16] Another finding is that conduct disorder—consisting of lying, destructive acts, undue aggression, stealing, and truancy from school—is found predominantly in boys. Severe parental discord is so important that it is strongly associated with conduct disorders even when the home is unbroken.[17] [18]

REFERENCES
[1] Davies, D L, *British Journal of Preventive Social Medicine*, 1956, **10**, 123.
[2] Bowlby, J, *Attachment and Loss*, vol 1. London, Hogarth Press, 1969.
[3] Bowlby, J, *Attachment and Loss*, vol 2, London, Hogarth Press, 1973.
[4] Shepherd, M, *et al*, *Psychiatric Illness in General Practice*. London, Oxford University Press, 1966.
[5] Chester, R, *British Journal of Preventive Social Medicine*, 1971, **25**, 231.
[6] Briscoe, C W, *Archives of General Psychiatry*, 1973, **29**, 119.
[7] Paykel, E S, *et al*, *Archives of General Psychiatry*, 1969, **21**, 753.
[8] Kessel, N, *British Medical Journal*, 1965, **2**, 1265.
[9] Bancroft, J, *et al*, *Psychological Medicine*, 1977, **7**, 289.
[10] Bagley, C, and Greer, S, *British Journal of Psychiatry*, 1971, **119**, 515.
[11] Morgan, H G, *British Journal of Psychiatry*, 1976, **128**, 361.
[12] World Health Organisation, *Prevention of Suicide*. Geneva, WHO, 1968.
[13] Baraclough, B M, *et al*, *British Journal of Psychiatry*, 1974, **125**, 355.
[14] Richman, N, *British Journal of Psychiatry*, 1977, **131**, 523.
[15] Rutter, M, *Proceedings of the Royal Society of Medicine*, 1973, **66**, 1221.
[16] Graham, P, and Rutter, M, *Proceedings of the Royal Society of Medicine*, 1973, **66**, 1226.
[17] McCord, W, and McCord, J, *Origins of Crime: a New Evaluation of the Cambridge-Somerville Study*. New York, Columbia University Press, 1959.
[18] Rutter, M L, *Journal of Child Psychology and Psychiatry*, 1971, **12**, 233.

2 Definition and extent of marital pathology

Any definition of marital pathology must consider both the stability and the quality of a marriage. Appreciable conflict or alienated indifference produce marital pathology, as do repeated departures and a final separation. But marriages where a couple never stop arguing, or where affection, companionship, and sex have ceased, may be stable; the marriage bond survives and has a meaning for the couple.[1] Thus marital pathology exists when the minimum needs of one or both partners are not met. Then separation and divorce are contemplated, and eventually realised, unless change occurs.

INTERNATIONAL CHARACTER OF DIVORCE

Marital problems occur in every Western society. A study of marital problems in Finland, Sweden, Norway, England and Wales, the Netherlands, Belgium, France, the Federal Republic of Germany, Switzerland, Austria, and Italy showed that divorce was increasingly common in every country, and suggested that the causes were similar everywhere.[2] Most of the countries showed a rise in incidence after the second world war, a decline in the '50s, and then a constant upward trend after 1960. This is inexplicable in purely national terms, and must have to do with changes in the nature of marriage and the family in Europe.[2] Similar trends are seen in the United States.[3] Is this phenomenon, however, extending beyond countries with Western cultures? Divorce is increasing among the elite in Lagos, the capital of Nigeria.[4] The special circumstances in Lagos include the Nigerian civil war (1967-70) but other factors appear to be similar to those in Western societies.

MARITAL BREAKDOWN IN ENGLAND AND WALES

The statistics of marital breakdown are expressed in several ways in England and Wales. The first is through decrees made absolute. Divorce has been increasing ever since it became available in 1857. Before the second world war, however, divorce decrees granted annually never exceeded 10 000. Then the divorce rate peaked after the war because of the vulnerability of war marriages. The rate subsided by 1960, since when it has increased again, and surged in 1971, when the Divorce Law Reform Act came into operation (table 1).[5]

A second statistical expression of marital breakdown is the number of petitions filed annually for divorce. Some are withdrawn or postponed, and rarely they are not granted. Petitions show, as expected, the same rise as actual divorces. Given that divorce rates for 1971-3 continue indefinitely—which is the case so far—and that marriage continues at the current rate (there has, in fact, been a slight fall),

6

Definition and extent of marital pathology

TABLE I—*Divorce decrees made absolute in England and Wales from 1940-77*

Year								Number of decrees made absolute (in thousands)
1940	..	..	..	..	..	..	..	7·6
1950	..	..	..	..	..	..	..	30·3
1960	..	..	..	..	..	..	..	23·4
1970	..	..	..	..	..	..	..	58·2
1971	..	..	..	..	..	..	..	74·4
1972	..	..	..	..	..	..	..	119·0
1973	..	..	..	..	..	..	..	106·0
1974	..	..	..	..	..	..	..	113·5
1975	..	..	..	..	..	..	..	120·5
1976	..	..	..	..	..	..	..	126·7
1977	..	..	..	..	..	..	..	128·0

then 22% of all women would divorce at least once by age 45. Thus roughly one in four marriages is heading for dissolution.[5] The total number of people divorced is a third expression of the problem. From when divorce was introduced in 1857 it was almost a century before the first million people were divorced. The second million was reached in only a further 15 years by 1967, and the third million in only six years. At current rates, some six million people will divorce during the remaining years of this century.[6]

DIVORCE AND CHILDREN

Divorcing couples who were childless fell from 33% of the total in 1960 to 25% in 1973. In 1960 divorcing couples, excluding the childless, had an average of 2·0 children but by 1973 this had risen to 2·3. At one time childlessness was thought to be related to marital breakdown.[7] [8] This view was severely criticised [9] and present evidence does not favour it.[10] But evidence exists that large families produce stress. Rates of physical and mental ill health increase with family size, and a critical point is reached with four children.[11] The mothers of families in Aberdeen with four or more children come twice as often from large families, often marry in their teens after knowing their husband for less than a year, often have a premarital conception, and, not surprisingly, often experience marital discord.[12] Large families, however, are not common, and their contribution to marital breakdown is small. More importantly, marrying and conceiving early are associated with divorce.

The Finer report estimated that in April 1971 620 000 one-parent families with one million children existed. Of these families, 100 000 were motherless and the other 520 000 fatherless. Of the fatherless families, 190 000 were separated, 120 000 were divorced, and 90 000 single. One-parent families formed about one-tenth of all families

7

with children.[13] Current estimates suggest that 750 000 families with one and a quarter million children have only one parent.[14] The social and psychological privation of one-parent families is considerable. In the United States, of the 10 million children living in one-parent homes more than one-third live with a divorced parent, about twice the number living in a home broken by death.[15]

TIMING OF MARITAL BREAKDOWN

Table II shows that nearly half of all divorces occur in the first nine years of marriage.[16] This vulnerability of the early years of marriage is supported by other evidence. One study in the United States showed that the third year of marriage produced more divorces than any other.[17] Another study found that most separations occur during the first year of marriage, and most divorces within three years.[18] A more extensive study in Sweden, that calculated the annual risk of divorce up to 40 years after marriage, showed that divorce increased from the time of marriage to a maximum after four years.[19]

TABLE II—*Percentage of divorces occurring after different durations of marriage*

Duration of marriage (years)			% of all divorces			
			1951	1961	1971	1974
<4	..	..	10·3	11·3	13·4	16·5
5– 9	..	..	31·5	30·6	30·5	29·8
10–14	..	..	24·4	22·9	19·4	18·6
15–19	..	..	14·1	13·9	12·9	13·0
>20	..	..	19·7	21·2	24·2	22·1

Divorce usually occurs, however, some time after the couple have stopped living together, and, as already described, the period between break-up and reconstruction of personal relationships is a crucial one for the individual.[20] One study found that in two-thirds of 805 divorces a delay of at least two years occurred between separation and divorce; for a third it was greater than four years; and the median was 2·9 years.[21] This same study also showed that in two-fifths of these divorces the marriage effectively ended in the first five years. Another study has shown that for divorces occurring in the first 20 years or more of marriage the start of major marital problems occurred for half of the couples in the first five years of marriage.[22] Thus, although marital breakdown may occur at any time, the early years are crucial.

No research has been done on the impact of preventive and coun-selling work but the early years of marriage seem to be the important time. This is, however, a complex matter because these early years naturally include a good deal of adjustment to marriage and this

8

adjustment may be confused with failure of the relationship. Research is needed to distinguish between these two groups; and, indeed, to find the most appropriate way of helping couples to adjust to marriage.

Marital breakdown continues throughout the whole span of marriage, and a sizable proportion (22%) divorce after 20 years. Clearly, while the early years are crucial, different factors leading to dissolution operate at various stages of the marriage.

REFERENCES

[1] Cuber, J F, and Harroff, P B, *The Significant Americans*. New York, Appleton-Century-Crofts, 1965.
[2] Chester, R (editor), *Divorce in Europe*. London, Martinus Nijhoff Social Services Division, 1977.
[3] *Current Population Reports* No. 271. Washington, US Government Printing Office, 1974.
[4] Iro, M I, *Journal of Marriage and the Family*, 1976, **38,** 177.
[5] Leete, R, *Population Trends*, 1976, **3.**
[6] Chester, R, *Politica*, 1975, **3.**
[7] Jackson, P H, *American Sociological Review*, 1950, **20,** 446.
[8] Rowntree, G, *Population Studies*, 1964, **28,** 147.
[9] Monahan, T P, *American Sociological Review*, 1955, **20,** 446.
[10] Chester, R, *Journal of Biosocial Science*, 1972, **4,** 443.
[11] Hare, E H, and Shaw, G K, *British Journal of Psychiatry*, 1965, **475,** 461.
[12] Askham, J, *Cambridge Papers in Sociology No. 5*. London, Cambridge University Press, 1975.
[13] Finer, M, *Report of the Committee on One-Parent Families*. London, HMSO, 1974.
[14] Leete, R, *Population Trends*, 1978, **13.**
[15] *Current Population Reports* No. 271. Washington, US Government Printing Office, 1974.
[16] *Social Trends*. London, HMSO, 1976.
[17] Kephart, W M, *American Sociological Review*, 1954, **19,** 284.
[18] Monahan, T P, *American Sociological Review*, 1962, **27,** 625.
[19] Dahlberg, G, *Acta Genetica et Statistica Medica*, 1948–51, **1–2,** 319.
[20] Murray-Parkes, C, *Social Science and Medicine*, 1971, **5,** 101.
[21] Chester, R, *British Journal of Sociology*, 1971, **22,** 172.
[22] Thornes, B, and Collard, J, *Who Divorces?* London, Routledge and Kegan Paul, 1979.

3 Social factors and marital pathology

Marital breakdown is a widespread phenomenon, which has considerably accelerated in the past 20 years, and occurs in most countries with a Western culture. Students of this phenomenon have asserted that common factors must be operating in each country but are hesitant to state with any confidence what these factors are. The factors responsible can be separated into two groups; general or global; and specific.[1]

GENERAL FACTORS

The first factor is undoubtedly the changing status of women, and so of relationships between men and women. Women have been starting to work in large numbers, thus becoming more economically independent of men. The husband is no longer the only source of economic support, and wives can opt out of an impossible marriage and still survive. This has also become easier because of reduction in family size, so that a mother can afford to look after her dependent children. This is not to say that the one-parent family does not face serious difficulties, but the economic climate is such that a woman is not compelled to stay in an untenable marriage. Furthermore, legislation has been passed to support her and her child economically in these circumstances.

A second factor is the gradual shift of marriage from an institution to a relationship.[2] By relationship is meant an equality of status and value and a diminution of fixed roles. The wife is not merely the childbearer and housekeeper, nor is the husband the main source of authority and provision. A deeper and wider exchange of feelings is possible.[3]

The changes in divorce laws, in Britain and abroad, make irretrievable breakdown the main basis for dissolution. This has indirectly underlined that society is accepting marriage primarily as a relationship, whose quality is most important, rather than a contract. Also, as material standards have improved, men and women are seeking more fulfilling personal relationships; their expectations of marriage have risen.

Another factor is increased longevity: some 20–25 years have been added to the expectation of life since the turn of the century.[4] Since marriages are occurring earlier [5] (a trend seen until very recently), marriage may last 50 years or more.[4] It has been calculated [6] that the average marriage lasted 28 years in 1911, and 42 in 1967. Some marriages now ending in divorce could have been terminated by death a few decades ago. Furthermore, this increased duration of marriage will not be buttressed by childbearing. Nowadays, the dramatic reduction of infant mortality [7] and the increased availability of birth control have combined to diminish family size. Even more important, on average women have finished childbearing by the age of 26 or 27,[8] which has freed a good deal of time for working outside the home. No evidence exists that the working mother is a cause of marital disturbance, or that she has an adverse effect on the children. An American study summarises the impact on marriage thus: "We find little reason to believe that employment outside the home either enhances or diminishes a marriage."[9] Similarly the evidence is unequivocal that the working mother is not a cause of emotional disorder of children, provided there is adequate substitute care.[10] [11] Finally, a major factor is the non-judgmental attitude of society. It is no longer a social offence to be divorced.

SPECIFIC FACTORS

Age at marriage

Most studies have shown that there is a close relationship between age at marriage and marital breakdown. Marriages when the bride is under 20 are more vulnerable to divorce. This is a finding confirmed in both the USA and UK.[12] [13] The much higher risk of divorce of young brides is increased still further if the groom is also under 20. There has, in general, been a reduction in the average age at marriage: in 1974 it was 22·7 years compared with 25·5 in 1931. Recently there has been a slight reversal of this trend.

Premarital pregnancy

Couples who have conceived before marriage are more likely to divorce than those who conceive after. Also couples who conceive early after marriage are more likely to divorce than those who conceive later.[14] [15]

Youthful marriage and premarital pregnancy

Further evidence exists that a combination of youthful marriage and premarital pregnancy is particularly likely to lead to divorce.[16] [17] From the mid-1950s the proportion of brides who were pregnant increased until, by 1967, 22% of all spinster brides (and 38% of those aged under 20) were pregnant.[13] But since 1967 there has been a sustained reduction in the number of brides pregnant at marriage. Birth control and abortion are important in this respect, and, since evidence exists of low usage of contraception among young people,[18] [19] abortion is the more important.

Social class, income, and education

In the United States there is a positive relationship between marital stability and socioeconomic status, and an inverse relationship exists between socioeconomic status and divorce.[20] [21] In Britain the results are similar (but not identical).[17] [22]

Age, social class, marriage, and premarital pregnancy

Teenage marriages are twice as common among semi-skilled and unskilled workers as among non-manual workers.[23] [24] When youthful marriage is combined with early pregnancy or premarital pregnancy, the conditions are ripe for divorce. In one large study the mean period between marriage and the birth of the first child was 1·7 years for teenage brides, but 2·4 years for older brides.[25] Furthermore, in another study two-thirds of those conceiving before marriage were teenagers; only a quarter of those not pregnant in the first year were teenagers.[24] The tendency for these mothers also to come from lower socioeconomic groups is shown in several studies.[26] [27]

Teenage pregnancy, loss of earnings, and housing

Teenage mothers tend to marry husbands with poorly paid jobs, and the mother's pregnancy often forces her to give up her job. If the wives themselves belong to the lower socioeconomic group, who lack occupational skills, then the financial disadvantage is compounded. This poverty makes it difficult to buy or rent a house, and compels many such couples (half in one study) to start married life with relatives,[21] which is well known to cause difficulties.[28] [23]

Thus youthful marriages, which predominate in the lower socioeconomic groups, often start with a premarital or early pregnancy, and are particularly vulnerable. Why does this happen? Many young people of this socioeconomic group customarily marry young: this is the way that they attain adulthood and motherhood, with their challenges and achievements. For some the marriage is a forced consequence of pregnancy; clearly a good deal of counselling and preventive work can be done here. And finally, for some unhappy youngsters pregnancy or marriage is one way of leaving home and parents.[29]

Premarital acquaintance

Hasty marriages are risky propositions. This is understandable because such marriages lack enough acquaintance to ensure sufficient common ground for maintaining the relationship. A unique study of 738 elopements found a happy outcome in only half of the couples.[30]

Engagement

A harmonious engagement could be expected to augur well for a marriage. A prospective study confirmed this expectation, and the authors claimed that their engagement success score was the only way available before marriage of predicting the marital outcome. Brief courtships of less than nine months, and stormy, tempestuous courtships are often a warning of an unhappy marriage. Broken engagement has been mentioned as a potential source of psychiatric disorder, but strong clinical evidence exists that repeated broken engagements suggest the presence of a personality disorder.

Attitude of the family

Since the Family Law Reform Act allowed young people to marry at 18, approval by the family is not needed, elopements are a rarity, and young people either marry or live together without a formal ceremony. Nevertheless, the attitude of the parents remains important, and some evidence suggests that persistent opposition by parents to the marriage is associated with marital breakdown, although the mechanism is not clear.[17]

REFERENCES

[1] Dominian, J, *Postgraduate Medical Journal*, 1972, **48**, 563.
[2] Dominian, J, *Christian Marriage*. London, Darton, Longman, and Todd, 1968.
[3] Platt, M, and Hicks, M W, *Journal of Marriage and the Family*, 1970, **32**, 4.
[4] Registrar General, *Statistical Review, Part II*. London, HMSO, 1971.
[5] Moss, J J, *Acta Sociologica*, 1955, **8**, 98.
[6] Willmott, P, *Urban Studies*, 1969, **6**, 3.
[7] Taylor, W, *British Journal of Preventive and Social Medicine* 1954, **8**, 1.
[8] Bell, C, *New Society*, 1971, **18**, 932.
[9] Campbell, A P, *et al*, *The Quality of American Life*. New York, Russell Sage Foundation, 1976.
[10] Rutter, M, and Madge, N, *Cycles of Disadvantage*. London, Heinemann, 1976.
[11] Wright, J D, *Journal of Marriage and the Family*, 1978, **40**, 301.
[12] Glick, P C, and Norton, A J, *Journal of Marriage and the Family*, 1971, **33**, 307.
[13] *Population Trends*, London, HMSO, 1976.
[14] Christensen, H T, *Eugenic Quarterly*, 1973, **10**, 119.
[15] Christensen, H T, *Journal of Marriage and the Family*, 1969, **31**, 209.
[16] Rowntree, G, *Population Studies*, 1964, **18**, 147.
[17] Thornes, B, and Collard, J, *Who Divorces?* London, Routledge and Kegan Paul, 1979.
[18] Schofield, M, *Sexual Behaviour of Young Adults*. London, Allen Lane, 1973.
[19] Peel, J, *Journal of Biosocial Science*, 1972, **4**, 333.
[20] Bernard, J, *Journal of Marriage and the Family*, 1966, **28**, 421.
[21] Ineichen, B, *Equalities and Inequalities in Family Life*. London, Academic Press, 1977.
[22] Gibson, C, *Marriage Guidance*, 1975, **15**, 379.
[23] Pierce, R M, *Sociological Review*, 1963, **2**, 215.
[24] Peel, J, and Carr, G, *Contraception and Family Design*. Edinburgh, Churchill Livingstone, 1975.
[25] Woolf, M, *Family Intentions*. London, HMSO, 1971.
[26] Gill, D G, *et al*, *Social Science and Medicine*, 1970, **3**, 549.
[27] Newson, J, and Newson, E, *Patterns of Infant Care*. London, Allen and Unwin, 1963.
[28] Inselberg, R M, *Marriage and Family Living*, 1962, **24**, 74.
[29] Dominian, J, *Marital Breakdown*. Harmondsworth, Penguin Books, 1968.
[30] Popenoe, P, *American Sociological Review*, 1938, **3**, 47.
[31] Burgess, E W, and Wallin, P, *Engagement and Marriage*. Chicago, Lippincott, 1953.

4 Choice of partner

Common sense suggests that marital conflict and breakdown are more likely in couples with little affinity for each other. The process of selection, courtship, and engagement makes it likely that a couple will share roughly similar attitudes, values, and opinions, and that they will sustain their common interests and avoid excessive conflict. The theory of like marrying like, homogamy, is well established, and evidence exists that if social barriers are crossed marital conflict increases.

PHYSICAL FACTORS

Measurements for similarity of physical attributes between spouses began at the turn of the century; they showed a positive but low correlation for stature, maximum span of the arms, and length of the left forearm.[1] Since then the whole body has been subjected to detailed measurements and a low positive correlation has been found repeatedly for stature, maximum span of arms, length of left forearms, head length, and colour of skin and hair.[2-4] The similarity of colour of skin is a reminder that race is a major factor determining selection of partner. In 1970 fewer than 10% of all marriages in the United States were inter-racial.[5]

Do spouses choose one another on the basis of a similarity to the opposite parent? Few studies of this exist, but one study established among 373 engaged couples or recently married persons a resemblance between the couple and parents, which was more than could be expected by chance.[6] The similarity in physical appearance was considerable, but more important was the similarity of opinions, personality, and temperament. But the influential parent was not necessarily that of the opposite sex. An important factor was the presence of strong affective ties between child and either parent.

SOCIAL FACTORS

Although physical appearance is important, the social and psychological factors matter more. In one major study of 1000 engaged couples, similarity was found in 47 characteristics, including religious affiliation, family background, courtship behaviour, mutual friends, and attitudes to work, sexuality, and children.[7] Common values make satisfying marriage more likely. A recent cross-cultural study related common values and marital satisfaction in both American and Japanese couples.[8]

Propinquity

Two studies in the United States have shown that about half of

14

the couples who met, dated, and married, lived within 13 blocks of each other.[9] Geographical propinquity seems to be less important among higher-class groups.[10] [11]

Social class

Considerable social class correlation exists between spouses, particularly at the higher end of the social scale.[12] Occasionally social class barriers are crossed and the marriage remains stable and successful. Clinically, however, it can be observed that a person with a high social status who lacks self-esteem may marry someone culturally and socially inferior as a way of compensating for lack of self-confidence. These marriages tend to be vulnerable because of disparity of social values.

Religion

Similarity of religious beliefs between spouses is also well established.[12] Work in the United States has indicated that religiously mixed marriages are more likely to break down.[13] [14]

Age

Reference has already been made to the increased vulnerability of young marriages. This vulnerability is compounded by the fact that a person in their early 20s is likely to marry someone equally young.

Education

Social class similarity includes educational similarity, but for education alone a high similarity exists, which is most notable in the upper and lower socioeconomic groups.[12] A detailed analysis of the relationship between age, social class, and education suggests that age at marriage is almost completely independent of social class and education, but that the latter two are related. Furthermore, similarity of education without similarity of social class is a more decisive determinant of marital choice than is similarity of class without similarity of education.[12]

PSYCHOLOGICAL FACTORS

Because it was so well known that people tended to select partners from a similar social background researchers assumed that the same applied to psychological factors, and the results of the earliest studies seemed to confirm this. Several studies of mental illness in couples concluded that mentally sick couples occur in the general population with a frequency significantly higher than to be expected by chance.[15-20] The crucial question is how this excess of mental illness among couples arises? Is it based on assortative mating—that is, unstable, neurotic people choosing each other—or is some other explanation possible? An exhaustive study in the United States adopted the view that neurotics marry neurotics.[21] This has been both confirmed [22] and challenged. Opponents of the view have proposed that mental illness arises from interaction after marriage. They propose that a couple do not start equally disturbed, but if the husband is neurotic then, at a later stage the wife is likely to become more neurotic.[23] [24]

It appears to be the husband's neurotic behaviour rather than his symptoms which contribute to the wife's illness. Such behaviour includes self-interest, dependency, emotional irresponsibility, and domination, and leads to marital conflict particularly over child-rearing and leisure.[25] [26] A more detailed Swedish study, confirming the British findings, showed that the longer a couple were married the more likely they were both to suffer from mental illness, and that wives are more susceptible than husbands to illness in their partner.[27]

Intelligence

Similarity of IQ has been found in all couples to a small degree, but is more important in social classes I and II than III, IV, and V.[11] Assortative mating among people of low IQ begs the question of the stability of these marriages. One study of 242 certified mental defectives who had married found that the rate of divorce and permanent separation was 20% compared with a national figure at the time of 14%. The crucial factor was the size of the family, and marital conflict increased with the size of the family. So an unintelligent but emotionally stable mother, who is not overtaxed with a large family, may expect a stable marriage.[28]

Complementarity

The usual view is that similarity, at least in social background, is most important in selecting a partner. Winch stood out against this theory and suggested that, although eligible candidates were selected for their similarity, the final choice was made on the basis of complementarity, in which opposites attract, and the needs of one spouse are matched by opposite and complementary needs in the other.[29] Considerable research has failed to give much support to this interesting theory, but clinically it is important because any change in the delicate balance between the complementary needs may cause a serious disturbance in the relationship.

Dynamic factors

Whereas the research of Kreitman and others has strongly suggested that spouses do not select each other on a neurotic basis initially, other workers think that, in fact, couples do choose each other occasion-

Choice of partner

ally for neurotic reasons.[30] [31] Perhaps one explanation for these divergent views is the use of the word neurotic. In one sense it describes conditions with considerable anxiety and tension, and in another, psychoanalytic sense, describes personality defects arising from development. Psycho-analysts postulate that beyond social and conscious psychological factors a spouse may be selected on unconscious factors.

Psychiatrists repeatedly meet emotionally dependent men and women who marry spouses who appear emotionally strong and reliable. These relationships may work for a time until it is discovered that the dependence is ambivalent: one partner is furious with or despises the person on whom they rely, or the apparently strong partner is an extravert who is underneath emotionally weak and needs as much emotional support as his or her partner. A person with poor self-esteem, who feels that he or she does not deserve attention or even love, marries a partner who cannot express loving feelings. After a while the deprived spouse becomes desperate for attention and discovers that the spouse, who was once acceptable because he or she made little fuss, is now intolerable. A man who has a poor image of himself may choose an over-critical, abrasive wife because he feels that being criticised is not only appropriate but the way to overcome his limitations. Gradually the absence of any recognition or approval becomes intolerable and the wife chosen for her sharpness is experienced as an uncaring critic.

Submissive-dominant, self-rejecting—critical, deprived—undemon-strative, insecure—controlling, secure—unreliable partnerships carry all the ingredients of dynamic conflict, as partners who are fixated, incompletely developed, or disturbed marry spouses with similar or complementary defects. For a time they collude: an unconscious arrangement whereby neither partner touches the damaged part of the self. But with change, development, and the need for greater intimacy, the unconscious bypassing of difficulties cannot be sustained and confrontation ensues.

CHOICE AND PATHOLOGY

Thus conflict may exist at a cultural and social level, and at a psychological level with conscious and unconscious factors of depriva-tion, dependence, and lack of self-esteem. Conflict on these different levels leads to the psychopathology, which in one sense is unique for every couple and yet at the same time contains factors applicable to most marriages. Stresses and strains occur in successive phases of the marriage as different elements of the personality are engaged.

REFERENCES
[1] Pearson, K, et al, Biometrika, 1903, **2**, 481.
[2] Susanne, C, Bulletin de la Société Royale Belge d'Anthropologie et de Pre-historie, 1967, **78**, 147.

Choice of partner

[3] Spuhler, J N, *Eugenics Quarterly*, 1968, **15**, 128.
[4] Harrison, G A, *et al, Journal of Biosocial Science*, 1976, **8**, 145.
[5] Duvall, E M, *Marriage and Family Development*. Philadelphia, J B Lippincott Co, 1977.
[6] Strauss, A, *American Sociological Review*, 1946, **11**, 554.
[7] Burgess, E W, and Wallin, P, *Engagement and Marriage*. Chicago, J B Lippincott Co, 1953.
[8] Schwab, E, and Schwab, R, *Journal of Social Psychology*, 1978, **2**, 104.
[9] Clarke, A C, *American Sociological Review*, 1952, **27**, 17.
[10] Coleman, D A, in *Genetic Variations in Britain*, ed D F Roberts and E Sunderland. London, Taylor and Francis, 1973.
[11] Girard, A, *Le Choix du Conjoint*. Paris, INED, 1964.
[12] Coleman, D A, in *Equalities and Inequalities in Family Life*, ed R Chester and J Peel. London, Academic Press, 1977.
[13] Landis, J T, *Selected Studies in Marriage and the Family*. New York, Holt, Rinehart, and Winston, 1962.
[14] Monahan, T, and Chancellor, L E, *American Journal of Sociology*, 1955, **61**, 233.
[15] Penrose, L, *Psychiatric Quarterly Supplement*, 1944, **18**, 161.
[16] Gregory, I, *Journal of Mental Science*, 1959, **105**, 457.
[17] Kreitman, N, *Journal of Mental Science*, 1962, **108**, 438.
[18] Ryle, A, and Hamilton, M, *Journal of Mental Science*, 1962, **108**, 265.
[19] Pond, D A, *et al, British Journal of Psychiatry*, 1963, **109**, 592.
[20] Nielsen, J, *British Journal of Psychiatry*, 1964, **117**, 33.
[21] Tharp, R G, *Psychological Bulletin*, 1963, **60**, 97.
[22] Slater, E, and Woodside, M, *Patterns of Marriage*. London, Cassell, 1951.
[23] Kreitman, N, *British Journal of Psychiatry*, 1964, **110**, 159.
[24] Kreitman, N, *et al, British Journal of Psychiatry*, 1970, **117**, 33.
[25] Ovenstone, I M K, *British Journal of Psychiatry*, 1973, **122**, 35.
[26] Ovenstone, I M K, *British Journal of Psychiatry*, 1973, **122**, 711.
[27] Hagnell, O, *et al, British Journal of Psychiatry*, 1974, **125**, 293.
[28] Shaw, C H, and Wright, C H, *Lancet*, 1960, **1**, 273.
[29] Winch, R F, *Mate Selection: a Study of Complementarity Needs*. New York, Harper, 1959.
[30] Dicks, H V, *Marital Tensions*. London, Routledge and Kegan Paul, 1967.
[31] Eisenstein, V W, *Neurotic Interaction in Marriage*. London, Tavistock Publications, 1956.

5 First phase of marriage

Married life may be divided into phases with different tasks, respons-
ibilities, roles, and goals; each phase has factors that induce major
difficulties. One of the best known ways of dividing up married life is
the Duvall eight-stage life cycle,[1] based on the age of the children:
stage 1, no children; stage 2, the birth of the oldest to 30 months;
stage 3, 30 months to 6 years; stage 4, families with schoolchildren,
oldest child 6–13 years; stage 5, oldest child 13–20 years; stage 6,
families largely young adults; stage 7, middle-aged parents (empty nest
to retirement); stage 8, retirement to death of both spouses. A shorter
classification has been proposed,[2] in which the cycle is divided into
three phases, and each phase composed of five factors: social, physical,
emotional, intellectual, and spiritual. Phase I lasts from the mean age at
marriage—which in 1976 was 25·1 for men and 22·8 for women[3]—
until 30. The maximum mean number of children for any group of
women born this century is 2·4 and these are usually born by the time the
woman is 30; hence this phase, which represents about the first five
years of marriage, covers the years before and during the arrival of
children. A second phase covers the years between 30 and 50, when the
children are growing up and leaving home, and a third phase from 50
until the death of one spouse.

The life of an American woman is similar to that of a British woman.
She marries at about 21, has her first baby about two years later, and
her last child before she is 30. Her last child marries before she is 50,
and she then has about 17 years with her husband before his death.[1]
The husband reaches all these milestones two to three years later.

SOCIAL FACTORS

The family tasks before the birth of children, which in the present
decade is being postponed, are to set up a home and share the tasks
of running it and to combine two working lives. Spouses have to
detach themselves from their parents and focus on each other. All
these apply to couples marrying in their 20s but special difficulties
exist, described in the last chapter, for those marrying in their teens.

Setting up home

Most couples wish to have their own home when they marry. This
is more often achieved by the higher socioeconomic groups and those
who marry after 20.[4] Those who eventually divorce are more likely
to share households, especially in these early years, and not to possess
a home of their own.[5] Without a home of their own, the couple lack
the privacy to concentrate on each other. Strife and conflict with
others in shared arrangements strain the marriage unnecessarily. If the

First phase of marriage

couple is sharing accommodation with relatives, then the wife does not feel free to learn by her mistakes. Frequent changes of home make it difficult for the couple to establish continuity. Making and breaking friends in the neighbourhood are also a source of stress.

Finance

Financing the home is usually a joint affair because wives often work before the birth of children. Women are now postponing child-bearing and remaining at work. At this stage financial problems are few, unless the husband is drinking excessively or is incompetent with managing money. On these occasions the wife has to take over the financial management, which she may resent. Women who are pregnant and out of work depend on their husband, and his incompetence is then a greater source of conflict.

Household tasks

An early requirement for the couple is to arrange who does what in the house. Traditional couples still exist where the husband is primarily the wage earner and gives minimal help in the house, whereas other couples share far more of the tasks. An agreement fair to both is essential. Problems arise when one or other spouse, usually the husband, after promising to help fails to do so and then blames his wife for being incompetent, or compares her unfavourably with his own mother.

Relationships

Withdrawal from the parents' influence, particularly of the mother, is important; the spouse must become the most important person. In-laws, particularly mothers-in-law, provide problems early in marriage.[6] The principal difficulty is when both spouses, but sometimes only one, continue to ask their parents for advice and help with crucial decisions and bypass their spouse who naturally resents being ignored. A variation of this problem is when both spouses attempt to disentangle themselves from their parents but neither can give the necessary support to the other to displace the parents. Conflict, arguments, and jealousy may abound and so arouse feelings of guilt and ambivalence in the child when the parent refuses to withdraw. These conflicts may continue throughout the marriage. Difficulties may also arise from the refusal of parents to approve their son-in-law or daughter-in-law, thus depriving their own child of support.[5]

Spouses bring to their marriage their relatives and friends, who may or may not be appreciated by the spouse. A few friends are lifelong and have to be integrated; others are slowly abandoned. Spouses may be jealous of each other's best friends, particularly previous lovers. Sometimes a spouse may pester for information about how he or she compares, particularly sexually, with a previous lover. In desperation lies may be told and the truth lost. Usually the important friends are integrated without such jealousy but sometimes either spouse—usually the husband—insists on maintaining both the friends and the pattern of his bachelor days, neglecting and excluding his wife.

Leisure

A long courtship will have ensured some approximation of interests but these need not be identical. What is required, at all times but especially early in marriage, is time together. Some husbands refuse to entertain or go out with their wives. Some wives will go only to her relatives and friends. Different socioeconomic groups have different patterns of leisure, but some shared activity is important for all. The wife may also expect her husband to help practically in the home, particularly if he is skilled. A reluctant husband may show his objection by taking a long time to start a task and equally long to finish it. The wife's anger is greatly increased when she discovers that her reluctant husband is willing to do anything helpful for others at twice the speed he does it for her.

PHYSICAL FACTORS

Health

The early years of marriage, before the arrival of children, are a unique opportunity to get to know each other. Rarely poor health intrudes and leaves both spouses little time to get to know each other. Also rarely a couple may marry after meeting in a mental hospital or home for the physically handicapped: the support they give to each other is crucial at this time of need. They marry at this stage only to discover later that they do not need each other or that their illness is incompatible with marriage.

Sexual

Sexual satisfaction is very important in these early years. Traditionally the husband has been considered to be the more sexually active, but the pattern may be changing, both spouses taking an active physical interest. It takes about a year for the couple to settle to a satisfactory sexual life. Workers in the US have reported that 82% of wives married for less than a year find their sexual life good or very good, and this figure increased to 88% when the wives could communicate fully with their spouse about their reactions and feelings.[7] That still leaves 12–18% dissatisfied, which agrees closely with an English study which found that 12–21% of wives were initially sexually dissatisfied.[5]

Some of these difficulties disappear later, but it is in this phase that we find a combination of sexual problems such as non-con-

21

summation, premature ejaculation, and partial or complete primary impotence. The wife may respond with failure to enjoy her sexual life or she may develop her own specific problems: failure to enjoy or experience an orgasm, emotional difficulties, inability to relax associated with a high level of anxiety, fear of pregnancy, and, occasionally, complete disgust with sex. Wives may also complain of their husband's excessive sexual desire, and her husband may retaliate by grumbling about his wife's indifference. Wives commonly complain of their husband's failure at foreplay, which leaves them unprepared for coitus.

Sexual difficulties only rarely precipitate marital disruption; couples usually hope that matters will improve. Since, however, sexual satisfaction is an important part of marital happiness [7] [8] a continuing absence of orgasm or pleasure will gradually erode the relationship.

Extramarital intercourse in these early years is not common but does occur for varied reasons. The stable extrovert with high libido, and the unstable introvert with low libido who has strong inhibitions, feelings of guilt, and difficulties in meeting people of the opposite sex, are both likely to have extramarital intercourse. [9] Dissatisfaction with intramarital sex, a sense of frustrating dependence, and unresolved conflict all make extramarital intercourse more likely. The confessed or discovered act of adultery may lead to considerable marital upheaval and a complete breakdown early in the marriage. This is, of course, dependent on the frequency of adultery and the attitude of the other spouse. Reconciliation occurs if adultery occurs only once, or on occasions when the husband is away and cannot cope with the loneliness, or even when an early marriage has left an intense desire for further sexual exploration, which is understood by the spouse.

EMOTIONAL FACTORS

The newly married couple have to become adjusted to physical and emotional intimacy. Emotional communication requires increasing awareness, empathy, and ability to express and register affection. Common difficulties in early marriage are failure of communication and insufficient time spent together. These two problems, which may occur throughout a marriage, may introduce an ominous gap, which may progress to breakdown unless the couple can adapt to limited interaction. Patterns of sleeping and eating and the balance between privacy and togetherness must all be adjusted. One spouse may cling to the other who wants to be alone more often. The distribution of power and the resolution of conflict are emotionally important. Couples from lower socioeconomic groups still think that the husband should be the dominant partner but the wife should have a powerful say in running the home.[10] The clear-cut expectations in such a relationship often prevent conflict erupting. Conflict may occur more often in more egalitarian relationships until the couple adapt. Unresolved conflict may lead to verbal aggression, and then give rise to physical aggression.[11]

Evidence exists that emotional satisfaction drops from the beginning of marriage [12] particularly after the arrival of children. This is supported by a study of a divorced population, in which half of the marital problems had emerged by the second anniversary [5] and 37% of the divorced had separated by the 5th anniversary.

INTELLECTUAL FACTORS

Assortative mating usually ensures considerable similarity in outlook and education. It is hurried marriages that may bring together a couple with widely different intellectual capacities and interests, but this combination does not often cause conflict. Literature portrays the marriage between beauty and intellect, the beautiful woman and the scholarly man—for example, *The Browning Version* (Terence Rattigan) —and this does happen, though the increasing education of women makes it less likely.

SPIRITUAL FACTORS

Marriages of mixed religions are more vulnerable.[13] Conflict over contraception between Roman Catholics and partners of other denominations was a particular problem, but now that more Roman Catholics are willing to use contraceptives the problem is less important. Angry conflict may occur between materially motivated spouses and partners who place a higher value on life and people. Conflict may also occur between those who wish to save and the immediate spenders. Other economic or political conflicts are possible, but the greater the existing homogamy the less likely is serious conflict.

CHILDREN

The birth of the first child is one of the most important events in an early phase of marriage. The couple now become a triad; the wife has to learn to be a wife-mother; and the husband a husband-father. They have to rearrange their lives to cope with the needs of the child. They must balance the child's needs and their needs for intimacy. The parents have to allow the interest and co-operation of relatives— such as grandparents—and yet retain ultimate control of the child. They may have to accept a period of sexual abstinence. The wife often gives up work temporarily. She loses economic independence and contact with her colleagues leading to greater isolation. The husband now becomes the sole economic and principal emotional provider.

First phase of marriage

Fatigue

A study in the US of 1296 mothers with infants under one year found that they spent half as much time again doing housework as mothers whose youngest child was a teenager.[14] Ordinary experience suggests that fatigue is a problem for mothers with young children.[15] Modern technology has helped, but fatigue may restrict the attention the husband receives, adversely affect sexual life, increase irritation and conflict, and reduce the time available for leisure.

Depression

Serious depression needing admission to hospital is rare.[16] Transient maternal blues are common but the overwhelming majority recover.[17] But a tenth of mothers develop a depressive illness a week or so after they have given birth.[18] These women remain depressed for longer periods, lacking energy, feeling irritable, hostile to their spouse, not interested in sex, and inadequate in coping with the baby. Recent work[19] has shown that depression is much more likely in working class women who do not have an intimate person they can trust or confide in; are subject to a major stress, such as three or more children at home; are unemployed; and have lost their own mother when a child. Depression is a serious and common adverse factor in marital pathology, and needs urgent effective treatment. Evidence exists that the divorced do not have a higher incidence of postpuerperal depression but if they do have depression it lasts longer.[5]

Child battering

A controlled investigation of 214 parents of battered babies showed that premarital pregnancy, illegitimacy, absence of the child's father, and marital disharmony are all precursors of baby battering.[20] These characteristics are more common in youthful marriages.

Physical handicap

Does a mentally subnormal child affect the stability of a marriage?[21] The evidence is variable; one study of families with a mongol baby found marital breakdown in a third of the families and in none of the controls.[22] The divorce rate of parents of a child with spina bifida is about the same as that of the general population.[23][24] But if the child is premaritally conceived and survives, the risk of divorce seems to be greater.[25] Clearly some increased risk exists, depending on circumstances, and the doctor should bear this in mind.

REFERENCES

[1] Duvall, E M, *Marriage and Family Development*. Philadelphia, J B Lippincott Co, 1977.
[2] Dominian, J, *Proceedings of the Royal Society of Medicine*, 1974, **67**, 780.

[3] *Population Trends*, London, HMSO 1978.
[4] Ineichen, B, *Equalities and Inequalities in Family Life*. London, Academic Press, 1977.
[5] Thorns, B, and Collard, J, *Who Divorces?* London, Routledge and Kegan Paul, 1979.
[6] Blood, R O, and Wolfe, D M, *Husbands and Wives. The Dynamics of Married Living*. New York, The Free Press, 1960.
[7] Levin, R J, and Levin, A, *Sexual Pleasure. The Surprising Preference of 100 000 Women*. 1975.
[8] Gebhard, P H, *Journal of Social Issues*, 1966, **22**, 88.
[9] Eysenck, H J, *Sex and Personality*. London, Abacus, 1978.
[10] Aldous, J, *The Development Approach to Family Analysis*, vol 2. Athens, University of Georgia Press, 1974.
[11] Gayford, J J, *British Medical Journal*, 1975, **1**, 194.
[12] Pineo, P C, *The Family Co-ordinator*, 1969, **18**, 135.
[13] Landis, J T, *American Sociological Review*, 1949, **14**, 408.
[14] Walker, K E, *Family Economics Review*, 1969, **5**, 6.
[15] Wiegand, E, and Gross, I H, *Fatigue of Homemakers with Young Children*, Technical bulletin 265. Michigan, Agricultural Experiment Station, 1958.
[16] Protheroe, C, *British Journal of Psychiatry*, 1969, **115**, 9.
[17] Pitt, B, *British Journal of Psychiatry*, 1973, **122**, 431.
[18] Pitt, B, *Hospital Medicine*, 1968, **2**, 815.
[19] Brown, G W, and Harris, T, *Social Origins of Depression*. London, Tavistock Publications, 1978.
[20] Smith, S M, *et al*, *British Journal of Psychiatry*, 1974, **125**, 568.
[21] Gath, A, *British Journal of Hospital Medicine*, 1972, **7**, 82.
[22] Gath, A, *British Journal of Psychiatry*, 1977, **130**, 405.
[23] Dorner, S, *Developmental Medicine and Child Neurology*, 1975, **17**, 765.
[24] Martin, P, *Developmental Medicine and Child Neurology*, 1975, **17**, 757.
[25] Tew, B J, *et al*, *British Journal of Psychiatry*, 1977, **131**, 79.

6   Second phase of marriage

The second stage of marriage is longer than the first and spans some 20 years. During these years the children grow up, the spouses change in their personality, and marital satisfaction drops. A careful analysis of marital satisfaction showed a steady decline from when couples were without children to when they had teenagers, and then an increase to almost the satisfaction of the beginning.[1] An English study confirmed the decline of marital satisfaction until there are teenagers in the family and the subsequent rise, but this was not to the initial degree of satisfaction.[2] Since 60% of divorces occur between the 5th and 19th year of marriage,[3] these years, which roughly constitute the second phase of marriage, are of great importance. But other work has shown that half of the problems that result in divorce start in the first five years of marriage.[4]

Thus, when we study the problems of the second phase of marriage we find both problems continuous with those of the first five years and new ones. These new problems are not clearly delineated, but frequently include change in one or both partners, which introduces instability into the relationship. Once again the five variables—social, physical, emotional, intellectual, and spiritual—will be described.

SOCIAL FACTORS
During the 20 years from 30–50 most couples have a stable home; the few exceptions include social class I executives who are required to move at regular intervals. Regular change of accommodation may be stressful because the couple—particularly the wife—are deprived of the support of friends and relatives and have to make new relationships.

After the wife stops working she becomes financially dependent on her husband. The possible problems of this arrangement were discussed in the last paper. Occasionally marital roles are reversed and the wife goes out to work and earns more than her husband, which may make him envious. But during the second phase of marriage many wives return to work. In the 1971 census 70% of women under 30 who had been married only once were economically active at the beginning of marriage, but this had dropped to 28% by the 6th year and then climbed to nearly 60% during the second phase of marriage.[5] After the child-bearing years many wives gain economic independence, which supplements the family income and also gives them some autonomy at a time when the marriage is threatened with dissolution.

The working housewife is prone to undue fatigue unless she receives support from her spouse and children. Fatigue inhibits communication and sex life and leads to instability. Such fatigue, coupled with responsi-

26

bility for growing children, limits the time a couple have to themselves for their interests, relatives, and friends. They usually adapt, however, and, with the passage of years, relatives—and particularly in-laws—come much closer to the couple. Indeed, evidence exists that divorcees often experience hostility to their marriage from relatives.[4]

A particular problem of these years is upward or downward social change. Upward change for either spouse, but particularly the husband, produces adverse consequences because the husband may now mix with a social group with which his wife finds little empathy. If she worked hard at the start of the marriage to help him while he was studying or starting his business, she may now feel redundant, unwanted, and insignificant compared with his new friends. Downward social change may result from drinking, gambling, or chronic illness, and the wife finds the lack of support intolerable. Another important reason for downward social change is irregular and unsteady employment, which often results from personality and neurotic disorder; [6] hence there are likely to be other conflicts in the marriage when the husband fails to maintain regular employment.

PHYSICAL FACTORS

Health

Chronic depressive syndromes may follow childbirth and may have a corrosive influence on the marriage because they reduce the availability of intimacy, sex, and leisure. In fact, any chronic illness at the beginning of marriage may have an adverse impact on the relationship. But the consequences always depend on the resources of the healthy spouse, whose maturity and patience are tested. Clearly the more secure, emotionally stable, and resilient the partner is, the more likely are the couple to cope with the deprivation resulting from chronic incapacity.

Sex

Marital happiness is closely related to sexual satisfaction. In an American study of 100 000 women, 94% of the wives who said they were "mostly happy" described the sexual side of their marriage as good or very good, and conversely, 53% who reported a poor sexual relationship were "mostly unhappy in their marriage." [8] A British study found that in a sample of stably married women and men, 96% of the former and 98% of the latter claimed that the sexual side of their marriage had both started and continued in a satisfactory fashion or earlier difficulties had been resolved, whereas 38% of divorced women and 30% of divorced men whose initial sexual relationship had been without difficulties said that it had deteriorated later on.[4]

In this phase of marriage the sexual difficulties encountered will be

Second phase of marriage

the initial ones that were never mentioned and the ones that developed later. Thus in taking a history it is important to establish when the difficulties started. Apart from the persistent psychophysiological difficulties, what are the common reasons for sexual dissatisfaction during these years?

Attitude of the partner

Complaints made at the beginning of marriage that continue and become established fall into three categories. Spouses who subsequently divorce tend to blame the other partner for being "selfish or inconsiderate" (complaints mostly by women), "cold" (complaints mostly by men), and "cruel" (mentioned entirely by women). Selfishness and cruelty include: failing to show affection before intercourse, reaching a climax quickly without concern for the wife, making love when drunk, forcing intercourse against the wish of the wife, physically assaulting her before coitus, and persistent demand for an unacceptable sexual variation. The commonest complaint is too frequent demand on the part of the husband without consideration of the wife's feelings.

The coldness of the partner refers primarily to the wife who, after the birth of a child [7] or even without this reason, becomes less and less interested in intercourse and finally will not allow her husband to touch her. One of the reasons for this has been described as a sexual phobia [9]: the increasing reluctance of a woman to participate in sexual intercourse is associated with anxiety rising to panic as the time for intercourse approaches. Such a wife will not even allow her husband to come near her.

Extramarital sex

A single or even repeated act of adultery is compatible with continuation of the marriage depending on the attitude of the partner. Extramarital intercourse is, however, a potential threat to the happiness and stability of a marriage. Kinsey found that by the age of 40, 26% of women and 50% of men had had extramarital intercourse.[10]

Clearly such incidences do not closely correlate with those for marital breakdown. But evidence exists that those who divorce and who also had extramarital intercourse tend to experience marital difficulties early on.[4] The extramarital intercourse may either have precipitated the marital difficulties or be a response to them.

Relationship of partners

A gradual decrease in frequency and quality of sexual intercourse may simply reflect a relationship deteriorating in other ways. Thus sexual difficulties during this phase need careful evaluation whether they existed from the start of marriage or developed specifically during this phase.

EMOTIONAL FACTORS

The most common contributory factor to a deteriorating relationship is the gradual emotional alienation between the couple. During these years the possible patterns are many; described below are clinical impressions based on some of the commonest. Emotional difficulties in marriage may be defined in many ways: the best is an interaction in which the minimum emotional needs of the couple are not met. The factors to be considered are not arbitrary: they are a combination of dynamic and non-dynamic factors that combine to produce a pronounced impact on the emotional life of the spouse.

Trust

Few intimate relationships can survive in the absence of trust. Some men and women have a higher need of trust than the average: they may have had unstable childhoods or may have a low threshold of anxiety. Such men and women need spouses who communicate well and avoid uncertainty and indecision. They are expected to inform their partners of their whereabouts, arrive punctually, and behave consistently. Marital conflict results from one partner feeling continuously insecure, which leads to anxiety and depression. The other partners may feel controlled as they have to sacrifice their own style of life.

Autonomy

There is a delicate balance between independence and dependence, which every couple develops for itself. Excessive dependence on a powerful, assertive, dominant partner is common. This may suit the couple at the beginning of their marriage, but the submissive partner— often the wife—may gradually gain self-confidence and self-esteem and outgrow her dependence. Often the couple adjust to this change, but if the dominant partner does not recognise, or refuses to accommodate, the changes in his partner, then one of the commonest marital pathologies of these years emerges. The wife, but occasionally the husband, begins to feel trapped, denied her newly-found identity, treated like a child, and invalidated, and may become angry and aggressive. The anger may persuade the husband to yield, but often the message is ignored and the conflict increases rapidly. The wife gradually loses her feelings for her husband and withdraws sexually, and a vicious circle of marital disharmony is established.

Often the emerging spouse has an extramarital affair and finds someone who responds appropriately to her newly-found strength and the marriage ends. Sometimes the person is trapped between wanting

Second phase of marriage

and fearing to go, and becomes progressively depressed. He or she may attempt suicide to break out of the impasse, or repeatedly leave and then come back after a short interval. He wants his wife to change in her attitude and her failure to do so makes him furious, but he is unable to take the initiative and go, particularly if there are young children.

Initiative

Spouses who are afraid of being dominated choose partners who are kind, considerate, passive, and easily controlled. After a number of years the "dominant" person is fed up with the passivity chosen and provokes the partner to activity and initiative. Such men and women complain they are fed up with being in charge and want to become dependent on their partner, to be looked after by them. Sometimes this reversal of roles is possible; often it is not. The passive individual is bullied and blamed for the very qualities for which he or she was chosen, and once again an unhappy stalemate may result or the marriage may end.

Self-esteem

Some men and women enter marriage lacking self-esteem: they may be outwardly assertive but underneath they lack confidence in their intellect and appearance, are easily hurt or rejected, and have a paranoid personality. Such people often grew up in families where they never felt appreciated, and felt that a brother or sister was preferred. They may alternatively have had a normal childhood but lost self-esteem in their adolescence.

Often persons lacking in self-esteem choose a partner who is inferior to their genuine potential. They may marry someone below their educational or social level, someone who is unattractive, or, far more important, someone who does not communicate affection. Such men and women subconsciously need greatly approval, affection, and affirmation. Later these pressing needs reach consciousness and create conflict, which is experienced as tension, hostility, or depression. They want approval and affection from their spouse and do not know how to seek it. They may make tentative approaches which do not produce any reaction because their partners are themselves often unable to express good feelings.

These complex layers need careful and simultaneous exposition if the couple are to be helped. The person with poor self-esteem needs to be reassured that it is perfectly in order to accept affection; the spouse should be encouraged to offer affection instead of persisting in reproaching his or her partner.

Conflict—anger—guilt

Conflict leads to anger; some people find it easy to express anger whereas others do not. The latter find it difficult to believe that anger is not utterly destructive, feel excessively guilty after expressing it, or are afraid that their anger is so powerful that it will destroy their spouse. Suppressed or repressed anger not only means that conflicts are not worked out, but that anger accumulates and may generate anxiety or depression with considerable guilt.

Envy—jealousy

Envy or jealousy may arise early in the marriage, but usually develops later when the partners get to know each other better and allow their competitive, deprived feelings to be expressed.

All these patterns may be given an individual interpretation by the therapist. The various schools of psychoanalysis have their own individual theories, but they share the belief that the important intimate relationship between child and parent is repeated in the second intimate relationship of marriage. My description has been based on the theory of Erikson,[11] but other dynamic explanations may be relevant.

INTELLECTUAL FACTORS

The essential point of the second phase of marriage is that the deeper layers of the personality are seeking expression, which may disturb the emotional arrangement. The couple relate with parts of themselves which were initially undeveloped, unacceptable, or unconscious, and linked with guilt. The single most important feature of this phase is the change in outlook, attitudes, opinions, and values. Conflict may arise when the husband, for example, becomes predominantly occupied with the values of his work, which gradually alienates him from his wife, who feels housebound, preoccupied with children, lacking in intellectual challenge, and unable to keep up with her husband. Alternatively, such a man criticises his wife for her "stupidity."

Another form of differential growth is when either partner cultivates intellectual or aesthetic interests that separate him or her from the spouse so that gradually husband and wife come to have little in common.

SPIRITUAL FACTORS

When couples have different faiths there may be conflict over how to raise the children. Other difficulties may arise from conflicting attitudes to birth control, sterilisation, and abortion. These specific problems, however, tend to aggravate other difficulties rather than create major difficulties in themselves.

During these years the outlook on life may change. Either spouse

Second phase of marriage

may develop a simpler, less materialistic outlook, whereas the other, often the husband, continues to seek material advancement. The conflict between material and spiritual values becomes more evident during these years and may gradually separate the basic outlook of the couple.

CHILDREN

The primary school child may have problems that reflect mental conflict: school phobia, antisocial behaviour, delinquency, and feeding or elimination problems. The adolescent child needs to express his autonomy, which leads to normal conflict with parents. Considerable difficulties arise when parents are unnecessarily oppressive; their children express their frustration by getting into all sorts of difficulties, but especially sexual adventures. Depressive reactions, suicide gestures, and antisocial behaviour may also occur. Other adolescents are excessively dependent on their parents, which makes them frightened to face the adult role. Even when they do face it, some of them feel empty and lacking in self-esteem, and become withdrawn and isolated. Experiencing these difficulties parents may become united or, if they are having marital problems, the family may be split, with one person becoming the scapegoat blamed for the collective difficulties of the whole family.

REFERENCES
1 Rollins, B C, and Cannon, K L, *Journal of Marriage and The Family*, 1974, 36, 271.
2 Walker, C, *Equalities and Inequalities in Family Life*. London, Academic Press, 1977.
3 *Social Trends*. London, HMSO, 1976.
4 Thornes, B, and Collard, J, *Who Divorces?* London, Routledge and Kegan Paul, 1979.
5 *Population Trends*, London, HMSO, 1975.
6 Sims, A, *British Journal of Psychiatry*, 1975, 127, 54.
7 Pitt, B, *British Journal of Hospital Medicine*, 1968, 2, 815.
8 Levin, R, and Levin, A, *Sexual Pleasure: The Surprising Preference of 100 000 Women*. Red book, 1975.
9 Taylor, K, *Acta Psychiatrica Scandinavica*, 1978, 58, 80.
10 Kinsey, A C, *et al*, *Sexual Behaviour in the Human Female*. London, W B Saunders and Co, 1953.
11 Erikson, E H, *Identity*. London, Faber and Faber, 1968.

7 Third phase of marriage

The third phase of marriage lasts from about 50 until the death of one spouse. During these years teenage children leave, the home becomes an "empty nest," and the mother experiences the menopause. Generally marital satisfaction begins to rise again as the couple return to a one-to-one relationship.[1][2] Nevertheless, almost a quarter of divorces occur in marriages of 20 years or more.[3] Evidence exists that, whenever the divorce takes place, 30–50% of the problems arise before the second anniversary: after the children have left, the spouse—whose minimum needs have never been satisfied—feels free to depart. Difficulties may emerge during the thirties and forties as the personality of one or both partners may change and make the couple incompatible.

SOCIAL FACTORS

During these years the crucial social events include the husband's problems with his job, the illness and death of the parents of the couple, and the marriage of the couple's children.

Husband's job

Two major issues face the husband during this phase of marriage: the position reached in his work and retirement. From the middle forties onwards one of four problems may arise at work: promotion is not attained; promotion is attained but proves beyond his resources; having achieved success he becomes bored and feels the need to change occupation; or he becomes redundant or has to retire early. Any of these may cause severe emotional stress in the husband leading to a depressive reaction in which he feels inadequate and ineffective; this exerts pressure on his wife, who may be made the scapegoat of his work problems.

Retirement these days may be earlier than expected. Unless the husband is ready for retirement, he may become depressed and his general lack of contentment may be projected on his wife, who is again held responsible.

Spouses' parents

From the middle forties onwards the parents of the couple are likely to become sick and die. During the course of an illness a spouse may find their partner unwilling to have the sick parent at home or to visit them. This causes conflict as loyalties become seriously divided. If the father dies and a widow is left, her entry into the couple's home might cause a great deal of argument.

Marriage of children

Parents may have problems with their grown-up children. The

children may decide to have extensive premarital sexual experience, live with their boyfriend or girlfriend, and refuse to marry. The parents may agree with this or, alternatively, they may not and may then quarrel between themselves and take sides with the children to the detriment of their own marriage. In addition, the parents may disapprove of the partner their child has chosen, and this leads to conflict and unhappiness, particularly when the argument is between mother and daughter, who are usually especially close at this time. A particular problem exists in social class V when the teenager, particularly a daughter, wants to marry and does not have her mother's approval. The tie between mother and daughter is particularly close in this social class and absence of support is a great stress, and may make the marriage of the daughter more vulnerable.[4]

All these problems are normally negotiable but they act as aggravating factors when marital difficulties already exist. Normally, however, in this period the couple are able to relax and do things together, and pursue their own specific interests. Their earnings are relatively high and adequate until retirement, when these decline: then this may present problems in a minority of families.When a partner dies the main problem is not finance but isolation and loneliness.

EMOTIONAL FACTORS

Three patterns of emotional problems exist at this age: those that have persisted from the very beginning of marriage; those resulting from personality change in the previous phase; and those belonging specifically to this phase.

Problems from beginning of marriage

These problems result because a couple have never managed intimacy, resolved conflict, or adequately expressed affection, mutual understanding, and support, and have not had sufficient time together. Their sexual needs, emotional needs, social outlook, values, and goals have always differed. The departure of the children stimulates the dissolution of a non-existent bond.

Second phase problems

In the previous chapter it was pointed out that personality change is an important source of marital problems in the second phase of marriage; these problems continue into the third phase. A spouse may progress from dependence to independence and the partner refuses to accept this, or a spouse who originally deliberately chose an unresponsive partner may improve his or her self-esteem and then find unacceptable the unresponsive partner. Or a dominant spouse may find the burden of being in control intolerable and want to be looked after, to lean rather than be leaned upon. All these changes may be seen in the forties and early fifties and lead to upheaval in the marriage.

Third phase problems

Often in the third phase, after the departure of the children, a gradual alienation and separation of the couple appear. They have slept, eaten, and lived together for twenty or more years with the impression that all was well. Yet they failed to realise that their only communication was through the children, and, when these leave, nothing remains to unite them. They look at one another and find they are looking at strangers. There is no conflict or hostility but an awareness that little else but habit holds them together.

No problems

The majority of couples in the third phase enjoy their marriage. Companionship and sharing leisure activities are important.[56] Gradually the married life of their children becomes an important part of their own lives, especially with the arrival of grandchildren; they may take care of their grandchildren and allow their daughter to go to work.[7]

SEXUAL FACTORS

The sexual life of the couple in this phase has been extensively examined. For centuries sex was primarily for procreation; a couple married, procreated, and, when their children were ready to repeat the cycle, died. During this century the pattern has changed enormously. Couples rarely have sex consciously and deliberately to procreate. Sex unites a couple and so extends after the menopause until the death of one spouse.

Early work has shown that although the frequency of intercourse declines with age the frequency of orgasm remains high. Other work has shown that well-adjusted couples continue sexual activity into their seventies and eighties.[8] Why does sexual activity cease?

Women

A small group of women exist who have never had an orgasm during intercourse and do not enjoy sex with their husband. Kinsey estimated that this was the case in 11% of women after 20 years of marriage.[9] But some women who have never had an orgasm with their spouse may do so with other men. A deteriorating emotional relationship may cause sexual activity to cease. The menopause has no effect on the frequency or enjoyment of sexual intercourse, but wives with existing premenopausal sexual problems may use the menopause as a reason for dissatisfaction with their marriage.[10] One study found that women in this age group (40–55) attending a gynaecological clinic were more commonly separated or divorced.[11] Similarly hysterectomy need not interrupt sexual activity. Hysterectomy may be used as an excuse for cessation of sexual activity; some indirect evidence supports this—thus women with various complaints referred to psychiatrists after hysterectomy showed a high incidence of marital disruption.[12] But local disease, neoplasms, reduced lubrication, poor surgical techniques for various operations, and vaginismus may all cause sexual difficulties.

Male

Persistent unresolved problems from the beginning of marriage may lead to intercourse ceasing in this phase of marriage. But the most likely thing to cause sexual activity to cease is impotence arising for the first time in these years. Longstanding evidence suggests that biological factors are operating and persistent impotence is associated with aging. Kinsey found that 6·7% of men were permanently impotent by 50, 18·4% by 60, 27% by 70, and 75% by 80.[13] Sometimes permanent impotence may come in the forties: these men have always had a low sexual drive and intercourse has been infrequent.[14] As they have no desire for sex, these men do not seek help of their own accord: their spouses urge them to seek help. Nevertheless, the prognosis is poor when the impotence has been continuous for three to five years.[15-17]

The wife needs to understand the nature of the impotence so that her anxieties about her husband's feelings towards her or that he is having an extramarital relationship may be allayed. A few cases of impotence are organic or drug induced, and reversible causes, particularly associated with the wide use of psychotropic and hypotensive drugs, should be kept in mind. In particular affective illness, such as depression, is common at this age and sexual activity may be diminished both by the illness and by the drugs used.

Adultery

Aging may create anxiety about sexual effectiveness. The fear of losing attractiveness or sexual capacity may lead to extramarital sexual behaviour. Adultery may also result from a deteriorating marital relationship. In one study in the US, half of the husbands whose children had left home expressed a desire for extramarital affairs, and a quarter had had one.[18] Poor marital satisfaction is usually the husband's reason, but not always the wife's. In one study, again in the US, about one-third of all wives had had extramarital affairs. The reasons were dissatisfaction with the marriage and sexual life: a few were satisfied with their marriage but did not regard faithfulness as part of the commitment.[19] As in all stages of marriage, adultery may result from marital dissatisfaction and gradually lead to marital breakdown or

Third phase of marriage

produce a crisis that may allow reconstruction of the relationship. Alternatively adultery may be tolerated; in general, however, it poses a threat to the marriage.

INTELLECTUAL FACTORS

A couple tend to retain the same intellectual interests throughout their marriage. A wide diversity of interests may allow the couple during these years to take separate holidays, pursue new interests, and generally go their separate ways. In the course of these changing values and interests they may find other men and women who share their interests and form extramarital friendships.

SPIRITUAL FACTORS

These are the years in which men and women gradually transform their experience into wisdom. Such a transformation may change their opinions, values, and goals. It may lead to a desire by either spouse to change his or her work for a more humanitarian, caring occupation. The desire to serve others is intensified and, if the values are not shared by both spouses, the unconverted partner may scoff at the new values and refuse to be associated with them. Such differences may also divide the couple when they are asked by their teenage and adult children to look at and approve new sexual standards. One parent may approve and the other violently disapprove, leading to conflict.

Change may lead in the opposite direction—namely, to abandoning religious practice by one partner, who finds that formal religion is no longer meaningful. A sense of separateness enters the marriage under these circumstances.

Both intellectual and spiritual disagreements are not enough to disrupt a marriage unless they are fundamental and irreconcilable. They may aggravate, however, an already vulnerable marriage and provide the final reason for a break.

Death of spouse

The third phase ends with the death of one spouse. If marital conflict existed right to the time of the death, the bereaved partner will have to work out both the normal feelings of distress and the remembered ambivalence of the relationship.

REFERENCES

[1] Rollins, B C, *Journal of Marriage and the Family*, 1974, **36**, 271.
[2] Walker, C, *Equalities and Inequalities in Family Life*. London, Academic Press, 1977.
[3] *Social Trends*. London, HMSO, 1976.
[4] Thornes, B, and Collard, J, *Who Divorces?* London, Routledge and Kegan Paul, 1979.
[5] Hayes, M P, and Sinnett, N, *Journal of Home Economics*, 1971, **63**, 669.

Third phase of marriage

[6] Orthner, D K, *Journal of Marriage and the Family*, 1975, **37**, 91.
[7] Havighurst, R J, *Unpublished manuscript*, University of Chicago, 1975.
[8] Masters, W H, and Johnson, V E, in *Middle Age and Aging*, ed B L Neugarten. University of Chicago Press, 1968.
[9] Kinsey, A C, *et al*, *Sexual Behaviour in the Human Female*. London, W B Saunders Co, 1953.
[10] Ballinger, C B, *British Medical Journal*, 1976, **1**, 1183.
[11] Ballinger, C B, *British Journal of Psychiatry*, 1977, **131**, 83.
[12] Barker, M G, *British Medical Journal*, 1968, **2**, 91.
[13] Kinsey, A C, *Sexual Behaviour in the Human Male*. London, Saunders and Co, 1948.
[14] Ansari, J M, *British Journal of Psychiatry*, 1975, **127**, 737.
[15] Johnson, J, *Journal of Psychosomatic Research*, 1965, **9**, 195.
[16] Cooper, A J, *British Journal of Psychiatry*, 1968, **114**, 719.
[17] Cooper, A J, *British Journal of Psychiatry*, 1969, **115**, 709.
[18] Johnnson, R E, *Marital Partners during the Middle Years*. PhD dissertation, University of Minnesota, 1968.
[19] Levin, R J, *The Redbook Report on Premarital and Extramarital Sex*. Redbook, 1975.

8   Marriage and psychiatric illness

Psychiatric disturbance is well known to occur in both spouses more often than could be expected by chance,[1] and appreciable marital discord and psychiatric disturbance are also associated. An Australian study showed that the highest rate of minor psychiatric morbidity was among men and women who were separated or divorced.[2] In an outpatient psychiatric clinic in the USA divorce was associated particularly with alcoholism but also with homosexuality.[3]

Several studies have also shown that marital stress is associated with the whole range of major psychiatric diagnoses.[4] Psychiatric patients who are divorced are also more likely to be readmitted within a month of discharge.[5] Thus a whole variety of psychiatric disorders are linked with marital pathology; some of the commonest are described below.

PERSONALITY DISORDER
Personality disorders include a variety of traits such as dependence, passiveness, aggression, immaturity, histrionicism, paranoia, and obsession; separately or combined these traits may impair relationships in a number of ways.

Dependence, passiveness, or immaturity may strain relationships in several ways. The first is when both partners share similar traits and pressurise each other beyond their capacity to cope. The second is when a spouse outgrows these traits and can no longer relate to a partner who was initially chosen to fit with them. For example, a dependent woman marries a dominant husband and later when she outgrows her dependent needs cannot tolerate his dominance.

A person with schizoid and paranoid traits finds it difficult to form a close, warm relationship. Instead he or she is suspicious of betrayal and often jealous. The combination of emotional detachment, suspiciousness and jealousy is particularly difficult to relate to.

Histrionic and obsessive traits are both associated with considerable anxiety. A histrionic personality has repeated dramatic outbursts demanding attention, makes accusations of infidelity, and threatens to leave. The obsessional personality expects life to be subordinated to order, tidiness, and cleanliness; pays little consideration to feelings; and often experiences considerable sexual difficulties.

Aggression links all these traits: physical or verbal aggression often accompanies personality disturbance and is important in causing eventual marital breakdown. One study compared 212 patients diagnosed as being personality disorders with 256 patients with undiagnosed illnesses: those with personality disorders showed more manipulative and impulsive behaviour, temper tantrums, and severe marital discord.[6]

Marriage and psychiatric illness

NEUROTIC ILLNESS

The word neurotic has come to describe two different conditions: one in which anxiety is the main problem, and another in which the patient has a disturbed personality. This section deals mostly with anxiety-laden neuroses.

Ryle found that neuroticism was associated with marital breakdown and poor marital adjustment, as measured by the gap between affection given and received [7]; Ineichen confirmed this.[8] Kreitman has also shown that male neurotics tend to be less affectionate to their wives [10] than a control group. A neurotic husband tends to lack reliability and be emotionally irresponsible, impulsive, and antisocial. He is also likely to sulk, make scenes, and be aggressive. Such husbands also resist their wives' independence, which thus restricts their leisure activities.[9] The inability of the wife to escape from her husband's constant neurotic behaviour may contribute to her marital tension. Marital tension is, in fact, associated with behaviour in the spouse that is either unilaterally dominating or segregating.

When one partner is largely dominated by the other the basis for this is often fear or dependence, which is often mixed with latent or overt aggression. When the couple do not relate to each other at all [11] they act independently over money, clothing, household arrangements, and leisure activities. Separate outlook and activity also lead to conflict and gradual alienation.

The studies of Kreitman and Overstone were in male neurotics; a common neurotic disorder of women is agoraphobia. Marriages between agoraphobic women and their spouse may show a complementary hostility and punition: agoraphobic wives tend to marry husbands who are likely to blame themselves rather than others for real and imaginary wrongs. Another group of agoraphobic wives, who were more hostile to themselves than others, tended to marry men who were hostile. The first group tend to be more disabled and married to equally disabled husbands, who show their disability in resisting their wives' improvement by developing severe symptoms themselves.[12] [13] Thus when an agoraphobic woman is treated and improves her husband may deteriorate and the marriage suffer: both partners should be treated. The onset of agoraphobia in women considerably reduces sexual drive.[14]

PSYCHOSES

Schizophrenia

Before more effective treatment became available schizophrenia was a serious mental illness with a grave prognosis that had an adverse and distintegrating effect on the personality. It would not be surprising if it had an adverse effect on marital stability. A study of 1295 women aged 16–49 suffering from schizophrenia and affective disorders, selected from admissions to a mental hospital between 1955 and 1963 and followed up until 1966, showed that some 18% of the married schizophrenics were separated or divorced on their first admission, and an equal number subsequently divorced or separated. At that time both percentages were well above that expected in the population. Also patients who remained for long periods in hospital were more often divorced or separated than those whose illness was less chronic.[15] In another study of married male and female schizophrenics followed up for five years, 44% of the men and 27% of the women had separated or divorced.[16]

A syndrome of morbid jealousy sometimes associated with schizophrenia is characterised by delusions of jealousy almost exclusively sexual. The condition is usually seen in men, although women are affected as well. The delusions consist of the absolute certainty of the sexual misbehaviour of the spouse confirmed by the "evidence," which may be stains on underclothing, telephone calls, telephone numbers in diaries, or innocent letters; indeed, the most bizarre evidence is acceptable. The delusions occur in a variety of pathologies including psychoses, brain damage, alcoholism, and disturbed insecure personalities. They tend to be enduring and can play havoc with the marriage. They may occur at any age but are often found in middle age.[17-19]

Affective disorders

In the study already mentioned of 1295 women aged 16–49 suffering from schizophrenia and affective disorders, almost 16% of the married women with affective disorder, which was normally a depressive illness, were separated or divorced on admission.[15] This prevalence was greater than expected at that time in the general population and almost as great as that of schizophrenics. But only 10% of women with affective disorders compared with some 18% of schizophrenics became separated or divorced after admission, which is a significant difference. Thus affective disorders are not so conducive to marital breakdown as schizophrenia.

PUERPERAL ILLNESS

Marriages often begin to disintegrate after the birth of a child, not necessarily the first one; this may be due to social factors. The mother may leave work and therefore lose economic and social support. Accommodation suitable for a couple becomes cramped and difficult when a child arrives. All this may contribute to psychological disturbance. There are also psychological reasons for a marriage to disintegrate after birth of a child. Evidence exists of higher psychiatric morbidity after childbirth than before it. Functional psychoses and depressive illness increase in the immediate three months after child-

Marriage and psychiatric illness

birth and rise again between the 10th and 24th months after delivery. Fathers do not seem to be affected in a similar way nor by events such as stillbirth, illegitimate birth, and twin births, all of which are particularly likely to cause puerperal illness. These differences suggest that, although both physical and psychological factors play a part, the causes of puerperal illness may be more physical than psychological.[20]

Whatever the cause, some of the depressive illnesses persist and are associated with chronic fatigue, irritability, loss of libido, and a general malaise, which corrode the marriage. Initially the husband makes allowances but after months, or sometimes years, good will is exhausted. The wife appears to have changed completely, leaving a shadow of her previous self. The constant irritability, lethargy, and loss of libido make the relationship extremely difficult and lead to a gradual loss of compatibility.[21]

ALCOHOLISM

Heavy drinking and divorce have been associated in a detailed study in an American outpatient psychiatric clinic.[3] The link between alcoholism and marital problems is well established, although not all marriages with one alcoholic spouse end in divorce. Wives may marry husbands who are known to be heavy drinkers, following patterns of heavy drinking in their own fathers. They may have the object of curing them. Heavy drinking may start after marriage and be associated with marital difficulties or sexual problems. In the course of heavy alcoholic bouts husbands lose their inhibitions and may become violent, particularly if they have pent-up feelings of aggression which they cannot express normally. Either spouse may turn to drink to deal with anxiety and tension, become dependent, and gradually damage the marriage through aggression, alcoholic behaviour, and loss of work. Women may also turn to alcohol to deal with rising tension emanating from marriage difficulties. Finally alcohol may serve as comfort after separation or divorce.

Much work has been done on alcoholism and marriage, and one study contains a good review.[22] The authors attempt to discover the factors that facilitate or hamper the return of sobriety within the family. They conclude that a couple have a poor prognosis if the following were observed initially: if wives gave and received little affection, or used few desirable adjectives in describing their "sober" husbands; or husbands expected little such approval. The prognosis was also poor if husbands participated less in family tasks, and used many hostile and dominant adjectives.

REFERENCES
[1] Hagnell, O, and Krietman, N, *British Journal of Psychiatry*, 1974, **125**, 293.

Marriage and psychiatric illness

[2] Finlay-Jones, R A, and Burvill, P W, *Psychological Medicine*, 1977, **7**, 475.
[3] Woodruff, R A, *et al*, *British Journal of Psychiatry*, 1972, **121**, 289.
[4] Schless, A P, *et al*, *British Journal of Psychiatry*, 1977, **130**, 19.
[5] Marks, F M, *Psychological Medicine*, 1977, **7**, 345.
[6] Jay, L, *British Journal of Psychiatry*, 1973, **123**, 685.
[7] Ryle, A, *Neurosis in the Ordinary Family*. London, Tavistock Publications, 1967.
[8] Ineichen, B, *British Journal of Psychiatry*, 1976, **129**, 248.
[9] Collins, J, *et al*, *British Journal of Psychiatry*, 1971, **119**, 243.
[10] Kreitman, N, *et al*, *British Journal of Psychiatry*, 1970, **117**, 33.
[11] Overstone, I M K, *British Journal of Psychiatry*, 1973, **122**, 711.
[12] Hafner, R J, *British Journal of Psychiatry*, 1977, **130**, 233.
[13] Hafner, R J, *British Journal of Psychiatry*, 1977, **131**, 289.
[14] Buglass, D, *et al*, *Psychological Medicine*, 1977, **7**, 73.
[15] Stevens, B C, *Acta Psychiatrica Scandinavica*, 1970, **46**, 136.
[16] Brown, G W, *et al*, *Maudsley Monograph 17*. London, Oxford University Press, 1966.
[17] Langfelt, G, *Acta Psychiatrica et Neurologica Scandinavica*, 1961, **36**, 151.
[18] Shepherd, M, *Journal of Mental Science*, 1961, **107**, 687.
[19] Vauhkonen, K, *Acta Psychiatrica Scandinavica*, 1968, suppl, p 202.
[20] Kendell, R E, *et al*, *Psychological Medicine*, 1976, **6**, 297.
[21] Dominian, J, *Marital Breakdown*. London, Pelican, 1968.
[22] Orford, J, *et al*, *British Journal of Psychiatry*, 1976, **128**, 318.

9 Management: Basic counselling

People with marital difficulties often turn for help to their GP. The GP must be able to respond well to this first approach, as it may not be repeated and may precede a suicide attempt or impulsive departure from home. The ultimate decision whether to continue with the marriage will always remain with the couple, but the interview with the GP may allow elucidation, clarification, and opportunity for reassessment.

People may seek help in various ways: straightforwardly by asking for help, or indirectly by presenting a physical or a psychological symptom. A person visiting their GP often feels that the doctor will only be interested in an acknowledged complaint. Thus, while investigating a clearly psychomatic or psychological complaint, a GP might ask some routine questions: "How are things in your marriage?" "Is everything all right at home?" "How are you and your husband getting on?" The answers may give a lot of information and may act as a trigger for the patient to pour out the problem.

A common problem is that only one partner, often the wife, will come; this is difficult because both sides need to be heard. The husband may refuse to come because he is apprehensive, afraid of criticism or being asked to change his ways, or unwilling to concede anything to his wife. It suits him to have her labelled as the "sick" one, as this takes the pressure off him: he does not have to look at his own feelings or behaviour. The GP can circumvent this problem by writing a letter to the husband inviting him to tell him his own story. If he comes, then it is not difficult to progress to a joint interview.

PRINCIPLES OF COUNSELLING

Counselling allows people to express their feelings freely, and to be listened to sympathetically without being judged. Anyone can do this with a little effort: it requires the ability to listen attentively, particularly to the feelings expressed, and at the end to avoid advice or judgment. The patients should be helped to clarify the main issues that are bothering them. Relief will be gained by expressing their feelings and having someone paying serious attention to them.

Counselling is much more effective if the couple are both present. The observer can see the way the couple feel about each other, the balance between anger and affection, the issues of conflict, the dominance or passiveness, and who takes the initiative: this allows the observer to build up rapidly a picture of the main problems.

RESPONSE TO CONTENTS OF COMPLAINT

For some doctors sympathetic and empathetic listening is not difficult, whereas for others it is a skill that is acquired gradually. Sympathy requires concern for another person and empathy the ability to understand and feel as another experiences him or herself. But what follows next? One of the strict rules of counselling is not to advise, which is particularly hard for doctors to understand as this is usually exactly what they do on the basis of their professional skill.

What is meant, however, by not giving advice is avoiding a didactic approach such as: "If I were you I would or would not do this or that." But the experience and style of life of the doctor may well not be appropriate to the couple seeking help. What is appropriate is to help that particular couple overcome their difficulties. Many doctors feel that they do not have the knowledge or experience to enter into the complex world of interpersonal relationships. But this may not be necessary as much marital disharmony is about three common complaints, which concern things, attitudes, and behaviour. These complaints may be part of complicated interactions, but sometimes they exist on their own, and by the counsellor simply drawing attention to their meaning a couple may be able to dramatically improve their relationship.

Complaints about things

In general it may be said that some people find it easier to express their affection by doing or giving things rather than with words, physical contact, or even sexual expression. Some spouses often accept and understand this, but others find the lack of verbal demonstration of love difficult. "If you love me, why don't you say so?" is a common complaint. Another common problem is when the husband, who is often the doer, starts something in the house and either never finishes it or takes far too long. This tardiness is made worse when he always seems willing to help others instantly.

Another common complaint concerns money. The complaints of the wife that she receives insufficient money or of the husband that his wife is a waster or incompetent may be perfectly justified. But, over and above such reality, money often stands as a token of concern and affection. "If he loved me he would not be so mean." "If he loved me I would not have always to ask." The lack of funds or financial independence can make the wife feel like a beggar, and the absence of a generous allowance gives rise to resentment and conflict.

Time may be a problem: in every marriage an optimum balance exists between how much aloneness and togetherness the couple desire. When these coincide all is well but when one partner feels, whatever the reason, the need for greater closeness, the persistent absence of the other is interpreted as rejection. This applies particularly in the early phase of marriage, when the spouses need a lot of support

45

Management: Basic counselling

from each other. The husband may excuse his absence and put his wife on the spot by saying, "I am working late for you and the family." In fact, this may be a rationalisation. He avoids spending time with his wife because he is more interested in his work, and the reception he receives on returning home may discourage an early arrival. Equally, if on coming home all he does is withdraw to food, television, or work, his wife has legitimate grounds for complaint.

Less often a spouse who needs more time to him or herself may feel oppressed by too much closeness. Also a couple can avoid each other by spending a lot of time in separate activities. Time, money, and activity command between them some of the most powerful means of expressing concern and affection, and a counsellor can help a couple understand their mutual needs and get the balance right.

Complaints about attitudes

Affection is expressed in the attitude a couple have for each other. Attitudes are formed in a complicated way from biological make-up and upbringing. A couple should get to know each other's attitudes during their courtship and finally select a partner with whom they feel comfortable, recognised, wanted, and appreciated. Most couples achieve something like this, but some do not. They may misread a partner's attitude during courtship, the attitude may change after courtship, or one partner's needs may change.

Spouses most commonly complain that their partner is undemonstrative and lacks warmth, overcritical, a show-off, restrictive, domineering, jealous, fussy about details, and rigid. A counsellor listening to these complaints must consider certain points.

Firstly, the counsellor must not take sides, however much sympathy he or she may have with one or other spouse. Secondly, the counsellor must consider how much of the attitude results from personality trait, which is unlikely to change, and how much the attitude might be modified. Thirdly, the counsellor must remember that often the attitude of both spouses needs to change.

There are many different types of attitude but the terms introvert, extrovert, and neurotic can usefully describe most. An introverted spouse will be described by a partner as undemonstrative, lacking initiative, and difficult to communicate with: such partners are not likely to change over night. But they can slowly change if their efforts—which are at first tentative—are recognised, appreciated, and rewarded. The counsellor must encourage this change by the introverted partner and ensure that the other partner recognises the change. In this way new habits can be established.

An extroverted partner in contrast is overdemonstrative, makes many promises, and is spontaneous and impulsive, but also probably shallow, unreliable, and untrustworthy. Again the counsellor tries to encourage the necessary changes, which are mutually rewarding.

A common complaint is of the spouse who is a show-off at parties and the opposite at home: often the spouse needs considerable attention, which is received at a party but not at home. Attention-seeking behaviour in groups by one partner sparks off jealousy in the other partner.

An anxious spouse may be restrictive, domineering, rigid, or obsessional; these are all ways that they can control their anxiety. Anxious people may control their anxiety by controlling others: to render them non-threatening or less frightening. When a couple gradually appreciate that their attitude is based on anxiety, much change can occur: the anxiety can be reduced with appropriate support.

Complaints about behaviour
The behaviour that is least acceptable in marriage is persistent aggression, withdrawal, or alteration of personality by drugs, (usually alcohol), illness, or brain damage.

Aggression may be verbal or physical, and needs to be distinguished from conflict. Conflict and its resolution are parts of ordinary married life; some anger will inevitably be expressed. Aggression is an expression of anger that continues and becomes the main type of behaviour. Marriages can survive frequent arguments, but severe verbal or physical aggression can be tolerated for only a short time. Such aggression can have many causes: an above average aggressive person; someone with a low threshold to anxiety, provocation, or irritation; powerful feelings of insecurity (jealousy and envy), injustice (exploitation), helplessness (excessive dependence), and rejection; loss of control through drugs, brain injury, epilepsy, or psychotic illness.

Anger may be transformed into withdrawal—sulking. Sulking may be punitive and deliberate or an inevitable reaction to anger and tension. Withdrawal may last a few minutes or may continue for hours or days; it is the latter which is so damaging. Such a person rarely apologises or forgives, and their partner must always accept responsibility and make the first move towards reconciliation; after a time this becomes intolerable.

Intoxication or brain damage, which may be temporary or permanent, may cause behaviour to become impulsive, uncontrolled, unconcerned, and inconsiderate. Things are said and done by a drunk spouse that are nasty, brutal, and frightening. A partner feels abused because the drunk spouse is no longer in command of his or her reason and treats the partner as a thing, not a person.

ROLE OF DRUGS
Persistent unacceptable behaviour, whatever the cause, is un-

Management: Basic counselling

doubtedly the commonest reason for marital breakdown and the most difficult to change. The same counselling principles, however, apply. The counsellor must help the couple change, with or without understanding the cause, by being mutually supportive and rewarding.

While counselling proceeds, one or both spouses may be experiencing anxiety, depression, paranoid feelings, delusions, or even a complete breakdown of the personality, and active intervention may be required. Many drugs are available to treat such symptoms. Drugs are best used to help a spouse to feel well enough to look at the problems facing him or her. Drugs should not be prescribed instead of investigating the conflict. Nor should one spouse be labelled as the sick one by giving him or her medication: this may reinforce the conviction of the other that they can do nothing so long as their partner is being treated. Rarely one or both spouses may need to be admitted to hospital to help them overcome a major breakdown.

TIME FOR COUNSELLING

Most doctors reading this book will feel that they do not have the time for this work. There is no denying that time is needed, and time can always be found if there is a special interest in the subject or a feeling that something useful can be achieved.

There is always time, however, to give the spouse the experience that he or she has been understood. What happens next depends on the individual doctor. Some may wish to allocate special time and continue the counselling themselves. Others may send their patient to a marriage-counselling service and then follow the progress. Some GPs have a counsellor working with them in their practice or work closely with a social worker or health visitor. Some have close links with a unit in a hospital that is interested in this work. Whatever the form of management, the GP should recognise the problem and then retain contact with the patient until there is a resolution.

10　Management: Psychodynamics

After a couple have expressed their feelings about each other, the counsellor must isolate what is causing the difficulty in their relationship. The difficulty may result from one spouse not meeting the needs of the other or one spouse not registering and using what the other is offering. What is the connection between such dissatisfaction and psychodynamics?

In marriage today a couple experience one another in a much more open, close, and intimate way than in times gone by. In the past a marriage worked well when a couple simply fulfilled their tasks or roles: the husband earned the money and led the family, while the wife raised the children, looked after the home, and generated affection. These roles were never absolute or inflexible, but if they were fulfilled society regarded the marriage as functioning adequately. But, in fact, even in the most stereotyped relationship the spouses had personal needs. In modern marriages couples try to rediscover the intimacy they have experienced as children. Modern marriage emphasises this intimacy, and much research has tried to understand this shift from "institutional" to "companionship" marriage.[1] The intimate relationships that last for a long time in the life of most people are the relationships between themselves and their parents and the relationships with their spouses. A person tends to relive with his or her spouse the important experiences he or she had as a child.

Dicks thinks that partners are selected in three major ways: firstly, people tend to marry partners of similar background; secondly, they select someone on the basis of conscious judgments and expectations derived from experience with their parents; and, thirdly, unconscious factors are important. Unfulfilled or fixating needs from childhood that have remained unconscious are aroused and seek fulfilment in the partner. Or unconsciously couples may match their complementary underdeveloped parts.[2] Thus couples can be helped by allowing them to express their negative feelings and then to look at their conscious and unconscious expectations of each other. The psychodynamics combinations of difficulties are numerous: they are described in the terms of various theories of human development. I describe here some of the most common presentations, but for further details the reader should turn to Dicks,[2] Sager,[3] or Skynner.[4]

The two theoretical, frameworks used mainly in this article are those of Erikson [5] and Bowlby.[6] [7] All dynamic theories of the personality work on the principle that a partner must undergo certain crucial interpersonal experiences. Mature growth depends on mastering the experience, enjoying appropriate parental response, and avoiding any distortions or fixations; otherwise the person may have difficulty

49

experiencing him or herself and others. This difficulty is particularly likely to be re-experienced in the intimacy of marriage.

Treatment has three objectives: firstly, to assess accurately which characteristics are distorted; secondly, to discount the defences employed to handle this distortion; and, thirdly, to encourage the ability to overcome the handicap and be able to relate more completely.

DISTORTED CHARACTERISTICS

Trust

The most essential ingredient for forming an intimate relationship is trust. Every young child needs to feel safe with its closest relatives; adults do also. Safety is experienced physically, and by being recognised, wanted, and appreciated. Sexual intercourse combined with love is a fusion of the physical and emotional requirements. We trust that the disclosure of our inner world will be received with care, sensitivity, and accuracy. Finally, trust means that we do not live constantly on the brink of feeling rejected or abandoned.

When one spouse lacks this trust, if the other spouse is sufficiently mature he or she can be helped to become aware of his or her partner's excessive needs and to behave in a way that will reduce the mistrust. Children may lose their trust as a result of repeated loss of close relatives, persistent unresponsive parenting, an atmosphere of parents threatening to depart, or several changes in the people around them. If both spouses have such mistrust, the counsellor may have to act as a reliable, stable figure who offers the couple a world of stability from which they can learn.

Autonomy

Every infant starts life by being totally dependent on mother, father, or an equivalent figure. An essential part of growth is the gradual separation and differentiation of child and parent. Every person must gradually become more autonomous: less dependent on parental support, and able to take the initiative and find a balance between closeness and separateness, aloneness and togetherness. A person with absent or retarded autonomy tends to choose a spouse who takes over completely or partially a parental role. Difficulties begin when the spouse who has the parental role tires of it and wants to be taken care of in turn himself or herself, or when the dependent partner matures and wants far more autonomy than is tolerable to the dominating spouse.

Sometimes parents are either so overprotective that closeness for the child is painful and stifling, or so indifferent that closeness is painful and arid: closeness is experienced as oppressive or rejecting. A person may react to either experience by becoming completely autonomous or compulsively self-reliant: acting as if he or she is totally self-sufficient and does not need anyone else. He is often angry when offered care and affection, which he rejects, and equally angry if he is left alone and ignored. The counsellor must help such a person understand the origins of his behaviour, and allow his partner to enter his life. The problem in such a relationship is timing: the spouse who shows affection or concern is rebuffed and withdraws, and so when the self-reliant spouse is ready to be approached the rejected partner refuses to co-operate. In this way a vicious circle is established. The counsellor has to help in interpreting the problem and in the timing of mutual response.

Anxious attachment

The person whose childhood was punctuated by discontinuity, unreliability, indifference, and threats of abandonment (real or imaginary) may become so insecure that all subsequent relationships are threatened by the possibility of loss and abandonment. The person may become falsely independent (as described), or he or she may develop an over-attached way of relating, needing constant demonstrations of acceptance, physically and emotionally. He or she is jealous, possessive, and controlling. The spouse is never left alone: he or she is pursued and his or her every move asked after. The relationship is stifling, and what appears initially as caring is seen as unrelenting intrusion and a threat to independence.

The marriage of two such unsure spouses rarely survives because they are trying to squeeze out of each other the security neither possesses. But lesser degrees of overattachment can be treated. One partner, using the counsellor as his or her security, has to "let go" and see that his or her worst dreads are not realised. Mature dependence can be developed: this means the acceptance of care from others without feeling destroyed if that person departs, which is the mark of immature dependence.

Self-esteem

To receive the care of others we need to feel lovable, and to care for others we need to feel that we have something positive to offer. As the result of an indifferent upbringing with poor or absent response from parents a person may not be able to feel lovable, wanted, or appreciated. Such a person yearns to be loved but feels unworthy of attention. Care and attention can only be earned and so he spends his life pleasing others without ever feeling good enough to be loved unconditionally. Such a person needs love badly but when he receives love he cannot register or retain it. He is generous and helpful in order to please others but in return feels used rather than appreciated. He is intensely angry with those close to him on whom he relies for his survival. Alternatively, he feels so needy that his very needs makes him feel bad.

Management: Psychodynamics

When anyone tries to reach him he withdraws because he fears that his excessive need will be experienced as greed or selfishness, and his anger over his deprivation punished with further rejection.

Such people are a challenge to the spouse who wants to reach him or her but is not allowed to do so. The spouse is faced continuously with a remonstrative, accusing partner who cannot be satisfied. Two such personalities find it virtually impossible to rescue their marriage. But less severely effected people can be treated: the counsellor must provide the means by which the individual can overcome his or her feelings of unworthiness, and accept the counsellor and ultimately his or her spouse.

DEFENCES

Psychological defences are used to avoid the pain and anxiety that arise from conflicts. Each spouse uses his or her own defence mechanisms to protect himself or herself from aggressive, instinctual, and affectionate needs and conflicts. Anna Freud [8] describes regression, repression, reaction-formation, isolation, undoing, projection, introjection, turning against the self, reversal, and sublimation as defence mechanisms. The common ones are: denial, "There is no problem; it isn't like this; you are imagining it"; projection, "It isn't me, it's you, it's your problem, it's your fault"; and displacement, "It's somebody else's fault". Counselling is needed to allow each person to recognise his or her fears, anxieties, aggressive feelings, and needs for affection and sex, and then to accept them as his or her own feelings for which he or she is responsible.

Revelation of a person's aggression and needs may make him feel so bad that neither self, spouse, nor counsellor can be faced, and he will avoid treatment: counselling is crucial at this stage. Insight into motives needs to be accompanied by confirmation that whatever is contained in the inner world is not beyond redemption: that greed, destructiveness, and badness are alterable. After marital breakdown a person often seeks another spouse with whom a fresh start can be made. This fresh start may be needed to avoid the feelings of badness or the demands of the original partner.

When reality can be tolerated, and it is the principal task of the counsellor to make this possible, the couple can give and receive affection and sex.

COLLUSION

Defences are a protection against unacceptable aggression, anxiety, or need. Another form of avoidance is to marry someone who will also not recognise whatever part is unacceptable or immature. Thus a spouse who wants to remain passive, take no initiative, and rely on somebody else, may marry a partner who needs to feel strong and assertive in order to avoid showing any need or dependence. There is a collusion or fit, which is often unconscious. Another example is the person who needs a lot of caring who marries someone who is especially caring, because he feels unlovable and tries to overcome this by continually pleasing in the hope that he might get some attention back.

Not all collusive relationships are fragile: most couples complement one another. But when complementarity is based on serious distortions of development then eventually the balance will be upset. Couples often seek help at this point when one person wants a change and threatens the tenuous arrangement. The counsellor has not only to recognise the components of the collusive arrangement but also to help the other partner, who may not want any change.

BEHAVIOUR THERAPY

Psychodynamic treatment entails interpreting the emotional patterns of the couple, giving them insight, and helping them to change through this. Behaviour therapy aims at changing the pattern of behaviour of the couple so that it becomes more rewarding and less destructive.[9] The emphasis is not so much on the antecedents but more on the present pattern, which is analysed to discover what the couple want and do not want from each other. Behaviour must be changed mutually so that it becomes more rewarding. The couple are given mutual contracts to reward each other when things are done well and to avoid unacceptable behaviour. Behaviour can be changed only gradually. "If you do this for me, I will do this for you." Much counselling is based on behaviour therapy, and provided the problems are accurately assessed much can be achieved.

REFERENCES

[1] Platt, M, and Hicks, M W, *Journal of Marriage and the Family*, 1970.
[2] Dicks, H V, *Marital Tensions*. London, Routledge and Kegan Paul, 1967.
[3] Sager, C J, *Marriage Contracts and Couple Therapy*. New York, 1976.
[4] Skynner, A C R, *One Flesh: Separate Persons*. London, Constable, 1976.
[5] Erikson, E H, *Identity*. London, Faber and Faber, 1968.
[6] Bowlby, J, *British Journal of Psychiatry*, 1977, **130**, 201.
[7] Bowlby, J, *British Journal of Psychiatry*, 1977, **130**, 421.
[8] Freud, A, *The Ego and the Mechanism of Defence*. London, Hogarth Press, 1966.
[9] Stuart, R B, *Journal of Consulting and Clinical Psychology*, 1969, **33**, 675.

Sexual difficulties are commonly associated with marital pathology.[1]
A counsellor who sees a patient with a sexual problem should discover
whether the patient is married, living with a partner, or living alone.
The counsellor must also assess the quality of the relationship. Sexual
problems are much more easily helped when a couple are willing to help
each other. If the relationship is good and the problem is only sexual
then the couple are more easily helped. Sexual problems are difficult to
treat when they reflect a poor or deteriorating relationship; attention
must be directed towards improving the relationship. A couple
experiencing conflict, hostility, and indifference may have a poor sex
life, but their relationship is the primary problem; indeed, one or both
may have a successful sexual relationship with another partner.

COMMON SEXUAL DIFFICULTIES

Non-consummation

Sometimes when intercourse is attempted the woman's pelvic
muscles contract and make coitus painful, which may ultimately
prevent it altogether. A woman who experiences this often marries a
gentle and unassertive man who does not press for intercourse if he
causes his wife pain. The counsellor can help the couple to relax by
examining their attitude to sex, contraception, and having children. The
wife is then encouraged to use progressively larger dilators, which may
eventually be inserted by her husband and restore confidence in
intercourse.

Dyspareunia

Dyspareunia is painful or difficult intercourse. Vaginismus may
cause discomfort at the entry of the vagina. Pain deep in the vagina
may be caused by a retroverted uterus with the ovaries trapped in the
pouch of Douglas. Lesions in the pelvis such as endometritis or sepsis
may be the cause. All these physical causes may be corrected after
making the right diagnosis. Psychological causes of dyspareunia may be
anxiety, apprehension of pain, and previous trauma; the patient can be
desensitised to these factors.

Anorgasmia

Primary—Primary anorgasmia, when a woman has never experienced
orgasm, is rare. Kinsey found that 10% of women had never experienced
orgasm by the fifteenth year of their marriage.[2] It is generally believed
that primary anorgasmic women have never masturbated and feel
extremely apprehensive about sexual contact. Current treatments aim at
overcoming this anxiety by encouraging the development of body

sensitivity and the ability to masturbate.[3] Primary anorgasmia needs specialised help.

Secondary—Women with secondary anorgasmia have been able to experience an orgasm and then gradually or abruptly lose the ability. The woman may have become anxious or lost sexual interest after the birth of a child, or her marriage may have deteriorated. Sexual arousal and response may always have been poor and may have been finally lost. Treatment may be psychological, or libido may be increased by giving 10 mg of testosterone daily sublingually for three months.

Secondary impotence

A wife's ability to experience an orgasm depends on her husband's capacity to maintain an erection long enough to arouse her. Secondary impotence, the failure to obtain or maintain an erection having done so in the past, is a common problem. Physical causes should be excluded. The doctor must assess whether the problem is occasional or continuous and deteriorating. Occasional episodes may be due to stress, fatigue, alcoholic excess, or depression. A man may experience an episode of impotence, become anxious, approach his next coitus with increased apprehension, and then fail again because of anxiety. The wife should offer reassurance and encouragement and possibly additional penile stimulation. The intervals between intercourse should not be allowed to become progressively longer as sex may become increasingly unfamiliar. A persistently low or deteriorating libido may be improved by erotic arousal through fantasy, reading, films, and audiovisual material, which may lead to masturbation; eventually the partner should be present and replace the alternative forms of stimulation.

Premature ejaculation

In premature ejaculation, which may also cause anorgasmia, the man reaches orgasm or ejaculation, or both, before or immediately after penetrating the woman. Anxiety is important in this disorder and should be reduced with drugs. The squeeze technique developed by Masters and Johnson may be used: before ejaculation the woman puts her thumb on the frenulum and her first two fingers on either side of the coronal sulcus and applies pressure until the desire to ejaculate is lost. This technique may be used as often as desired, and gradually the man may learn better control.[4]

REDUCING SEXUAL ANXIETY

Poor sexual performance is often related to anxiety; modern sexual treatment following the techniques of Masters and Johnson [5] uses methods to reduce this.[5] [6] This advice may be given without specialised training to a co-operative couple. A couple experiencing persistent

Management: Sexual counselling

sexual difficulties can be advised, as described subsequently, before they are recommended to seek specialised help. The difficulties may be infrequent or absent intercourse, non-enjoyable intercourse, episodes of impotence, or gradual sexual alienation in the absence of marital difficulties. The couple are advised to stop attempting to have intercourse: their sexual life must start afresh. They must first become relaxed when feeling each other. When relaxed, perhaps when on holiday, they can concentrate on feeling each other's bodies. They must aim through touching, caressing, and stroking to give pleasure. All this contact must be non-genital. When the couple are relaxed and happy with this non-genital contact, they proceed to genital play with intercourse still forbidden. Then the couple choose a sexual position that is easy for both of them and allow penetration but no thrusting. Finally full intercourse is achieved.

The aim is to achieve considerable relaxation and allow the partner to tell the other what gives him or her pleasure. The accent is removed from the genitalia. The couple learn how much relaxation they need, what parts of their bodies give them extra pleasure, the secure feeling of touching each other physically and genitally, the pleasure of being inside each other without hurrying to the climax, a small number of coital positions that they are at home with, and the right pacing to experience mutual orgasms or at least mutual pleasure.

Sexual variations

A wide variety of objects, words, pictures, fantasies, coital positions, and activities may arouse erotic excitement. The couple should be able to use their aids without guilt, and neither partner should coerce the other to do what they do not want to do. The couple must feel that they themselves matter more than the variation. When incompatibility is considerable then expert help is needed, particularly if the variation becomes the only form of sexual activity.

SEX AND MARITAL PROBLEMS

Sexual problems are often the first sign of a deteriorating relationship. The counsellor must assess the quality of the marriage before starting sexual therapy. This does not mean that sexual therapy may not proceed simultaneously, but sometimes marital counselling should precede it.

Marriage without coitus

Sexual therapies have made considerable progress in the last decade and a sexless marriage should now be rare, but it does exist. The sexual life of a couple who never have intercourse may take alternative forms of physical and genital stimulation depending on what they find acceptable. Sometimes even this alternative sexual stimulation will not be available. The counsellor must establish if a third person is providing the missing sex needs. The counsellor may be put into difficulties if asked not to divulge this information. He or she is obliged to treat this information as confidential. Telling the partner may be disastrous or essential: the counsellor can choose either to desist or to continue until change is possible. Nevertheless, he or she must avoid deliberately deceiving. But if neither intercourse nor other sexual variations are possible then the couple need to reinforce their affection for each other in alternative ways. Sexual intercourse is a powerful means of uniting a couple and needs adequate compensation when missing.

THE DOCTOR AND SEX

Doctors reflect the society in which they live and work, and, despite the greater freedom that exists in discussing sex, not all of them are either comfortable with the subject or familiar with the advances made. Doctors must become aware of their own sensitivities and limitations for they are often the first port of help for those who experience sexual difficulties. Doctors must only treat the problems that they feel capable of tackling and should refer others to marriage-counselling centres or to other departments that treat sexual problems. Sexual problems form a large part of marital difficulties and an effective early response may make a great difference to the outcome of a marriage.

REFERENCES

[1] *Aspects of Sexual Medicine.* London, British Medical Association, 1976.
[2] Kinsey, A C, *et al, Sexual Behaviour in the Human Female.* London, W B Saunders and Co, 1953.
[3] Riley, A J, and Riley, E J, *British Journal of Psychiatry*, 1978, **133**, 404.
[4] Carney, A, *et al, British Journal of Psychiatry*, 1978, **133**, 339.
[5] Masters, W H, and Johnson, V E, *Human Sexual Inadequacy.* Edinburgh, Churchill Livingstone, 1970.
[6] Kaplan, H, *Sex Therapy Today.* New York, Open Books, 1974.